The

Protestant Ethic

and the

Spirit *of* Capitalism

Max Weber

Contents

The Problem

The Practical Ethics *of the* Ascetic Branches *of* Protestantism

THE PROBLEM

Chapter I

Religious Affiliation & Social Stratification[A]

A glance at the occupational statistics of any country of mixed religious composition brings to light with remarkable frequency[B] a situation which has several times provoked discussion in the Catholic press and literature, and in Catholic congresses in Germany, namely, the fact that business leaders and owners of capital, as well as the higher grades of skilled labor, and even more the higher technically and commercially trained personnel of modern enterprises, are overwhelmingly Protestant. This is true not only in cases where the difference in religion coincides with one of nationality, and thus of cultural development, as in Eastern Germany between Germans and Poles. The same thing is shown in the figures of religious affiliation almost wherever capitalism, at the time of its great expansion, has had a free hand to alter the social distribution of the population in accordance with its needs, and to determine its occupational structure. The more freedom it has had, the more clearly is the effect shown. It is true that the greater relative participation of Protestants in the ownership of capital,[1] in management, and the upper ranks of labor in great modern industrial and commercial enterprises, may in part be explained in terms of historical circumstances, which extend far back into the past, and in which religious affiliation is not a cause

---

[1] For instance, in 1895 in Baden there was taxable capital available for the tax on returns from capital:

Per 1,000 Protestants . . . . . . 954,000 marks
Per 1,000 Catholics . . . . . . 589,000 marks

It is true that the Jews, with over four million per 1,000, were far ahead of the rest. (For details see Offenbacher, *op. cit.*, p. 21.)

of the economic conditions, but to a certain extent appears to be a result of them. Participation in the above economic functions usually involves some previous ownership of capital, and generally an expensive education; often both. These are today largely dependent on the possession of inherited wealth, or at least on a certain degree of material well being. A number of those sections of the old Empire which were most highly developed economically and most favored by natural resources and situation, in particular a majority of the wealthy towns went over to Protestantism in the sixteenth century. The results of that circumstance favor the Protestants even today in their struggle for economic existence. There arises thus the historical question: why were the districts of highest economic development at the same time particularly favorable to a revolution in the Church? The answer is by no means so simple as one might think.

The emancipation from economic traditionalism appears, no doubt, to be a factor which would greatly strengthen the tendency to doubt the sanctity of the religious tradition, as of all traditional authorities. But it is necessary to note, what has often been forgotten, that the Reformation meant not the elimination the Church's control over everyday life, but rather the substitution of a new form of control for the previous, one. It meant the repudiation of a control which was very lax, at that time scarcely perceptible in practice, and hardly more than formal, in favor of a regulation, of the whole of conduct which, penetrating to all departments of private and public life, was infinitely, burdensome and earnestly enforced. The rule of the Catholic Church, "punishing the heretic, but indulgent. to the sinner", as it was in the past even more than today, is now tolerated by peoples of thoroughly modern economic character, and was borne by the richest and economically most advanced peoples on earth at about the turn of the fifteenth century. The rule of Calvinism, on the other hand, as it was enforced in the sixteenth century in Geneva and in Scotland, at the turn of the sixteenth and seventeenth centuries in large parts of the Netherlands, in the seventeenth in New England, and for a time in England itself, would be for us the most absolutely unbearable form of ecclesiastical control of the individual which could possibly exist. That was exactly what large numbers of the old commercial aristocracy of those times, in Geneva as well as in Holland and England, felt about it. And what the reformers complained of in those areas of high economic development was not too much supervision of life on the part of the Church, but too little. Now how does it happen that at that time those countries which were most advanced economically, and within them the rising bourgeois middle classes, not only failed to resist this unexampled tyranny of Puritanism, but even developed a heroism in its defense? For bourgeois classes as such have seldom before and never since displayed heroism. It was "the last of our heroisms", as Carlyle, not without reason, has said.

But further, and especially important: it may be, as has been claimed, that the greater participation of Protestants in the positions of ownership and management in modern economic life may today be understood, in part at least, simply as a result of the greater material wealth they have inherited. But there are certain other phenomena which cannot be explained in the same way. Thus, to mention only a few facts: there is a great difference discoverable in Baden, in Bavaria, in Hungary, in the type of higher education which Catholic parents, as opposed to Protestant, give their children. That the percentage of Catholics among the students and graduates of higher educational institutions in general lags behind their proportion of the total population," may, to be sure, be largely explicable in terms of inherited differences of wealth. But among the Catholic graduates themselves the percentage of those graduating from the institutions preparing, in particular, for technical studies and industrial and commercial occupations, but in general from those preparing for middle-class business life, lags still farther behind the percentage of Protestants. On the other hand, Catholics prefer the sort of training which the humanistic Gymnasium affords. That is a circumstance to which the above explanation does not apply, but which, on the contrary, is one reason why so few Catholics are engaged in capitalistic enterprise.

Even more striking is a fact which partly explains the smaller proportion of Catholics among the skilled laborers of modern industry. It is well known that the factory has taken its skilled labor to a large extent from young men in the handicrafts; but this is much more true of Protestant than of Catholic journeymen. Among journeymen, in other words, the Catholics show a stronger propensity to remain in their crafts, that is they more often become master craftsmen, whereas the Protestants are attracted to a larger extent into the factories in order to fill the upper ranks skilled labor and administrative positions. The explanation of these cases is undoubtedly that the mental and spiritual peculiarities acquired from the environment, here the type of education favored by the religious atmosphere of the home community and the parental home, have determined the choice of occupation, and through it the professional career.

The smaller participation of Catholics in the modern business life of Germany is all the more striking because it runs counter to a tendency which has been observed at all times including the present. National or religious minorities which are in a position of subordination to a group of rulers are likely, through their voluntary or involuntary exclusion from positions of political influence, to be driven with peculiar force into economic activity. Their ablest members seek to satisfy the desire for recognition of their abilities in this field, since there is no opportunity in the service of the State. This has undoubtedly been true of the Poles in Russia and Eastern Prussia, who have without question been undergoing a more rapid economic advance than in Galicia, where they have been in the ascendant. It has in earlier times been true of the Huguenots in France under Louis XIV, the Nonconformists and Quakers in England, and, last but not least, the Jew for two thousand years. But the Catholics in Germany have shown no striking evidence of such a result of their position. In the past they have, unlike the Protestants, undergone no particularly prominent economic development in the times when they, were persecuted or only tolerated, either in Holland or in England. On the other hand, it is a fact that the Protestants (especially certain branches of the movement to be fully discussed later) both as ruling classes and as ruled, both as majority and as minority, have shown a special tendency to develop economic rationalism which cannot be observed to the same extent among Catholics either in the one situation or in the other.[2] Thus the

---

[2] Petty's reference to the case of Ireland is very simply explained by the fact that the Protestants were only involved in the capacity of absentee landlords. If he had meant to maintain more he would have been wrong, as the situation of the Scotch-Irish shows. The typical relationship between Protestantism and capitalism existed

principal explanation of this difference must be sought in the permanent intrinsic character of their religious beliefs, and not only in their temporary external historic-political situations.[3]

It will be our task to investigate these religions with a view to finding out what peculiarities they have or have had which might have resulted in the behavior we have described. On superficial analysis, and on the basis of certain current impressions, one might be tempted to express the difference by saying that the greater other-worldliness of Catholicism, the ascetic character of its highest ideals, must have brought up its adherents to a greater indifference toward the good things of this world. Such an explanation fits the popular tendency in the judgment of both religions. On the Protestant side it is used as a basis of criticism of those (real or imagined) ascetic ideals of the Catholic way of life, while the Catholics answer with the accusation that materialism results from the secularization of all ideals through Protestantism. One recent writer has attempted to formulate the difference of their attitudes toward economic life in the following manner: "The Catholic is quieter, having less of the acquisitive impulse; he prefers a life of the greatest possible security, even with a smaller income, to a life of risk and excitement, even though it may bring the chance of gaining honor and riches. The proverb says jokingly, either eat well or sleep well. In the present case the Protestant prefers to eat well, the Catholic to sleep undisturbed."

In fact, this desire to eat well may be a correct though incomplete characterization of the motives of many nominal Protestants in Germany at the present time. But things were very different in the past: the English, Dutch, and American Puritans were characterized by the exact opposite of the joy of living, a fact which is indeed, as we shall see, most important for our pre sent study. Moreover, the French Protestants, among others, long retained, and retain to a

---

in Ireland as well as elsewhere. (On the Scotch-Irish see C. A. Hanna, *The Scotch-Irish*, two vols., Putnam, New York.)

[3] This is not, of course, to deny that the latter facts have had exceedingly important consequences. As I shall show later, the fact that many Protestant sects were small and hence homogeneous minorities, as were all the strict Calvinists outside of Geneva and New England, even where they were in possession of political power, was of fundamental significance for the development of their whole character, including their manner of participation in economic life.

certain extent up to the present, the characteristics which were impressed upon the Calvinistic Churches everywhere, especially under the cross in the time of the religious struggles. Nevertheless (or was it, perhaps, as we shall ask later, precisely on that account?) it is well known that these characteristics were one of the most important factors in the industrial and capitalistic development of France, and on the small scale permitted them by their persecution remained so. If we may call this seriousness and the strong predominance of religious interests in the whole conduct of life otherworldliness, then the French Calvinists were and still are at least as otherworldly as, for instance, the North German Catholics, to whom their Catholicism is undoubtedly as vital a matter as religion is to any other people in the world. Both differ from the predominant religious trends in their respective countries in much the same way. The Catholics of France are, in their lower ranks, greatly interested in the enjoyment of life, in the upper directly hostile to religion. Similarly, the Protestants of Germany are today absorbed in worldly economic life, and their upper ranks are most indifferent to religion. Hardly anything shows so clearly as this parallel that, with such vague ideas as that of the alleged otherworldliness of Catholicism, and the alleged materialistic joy of living of Protestantism, and others like them, nothing can be accomplished for our purpose. In such general terms the distinction does not even adequately fit the facts of today, and certainly not of the past. If, however, one wishes to make use of it at all, several other observations present themselves at once which, combined with the above remarks, suggest that the supposed conflict between other-worldliness, asceticism, and ecclesiastical piety on the one side, and participation in capitalistic acquisition on the other, might actually turn out to be an intimate relationship.

As a matter of fact it is surely remarkable, to begin with quite a superficial observation, how large is the number of representatives of the most spiritual forms of Christian piety who have sprung from commercial circles. In particular, very many of the most zealous adherents of Pietism are of this origin. It might e explained as a sort of reaction against mammonism on the part of sensitive natures not adapted to commercial life, and, as in the case of Francis of Assisi, man Pietists have themselves interpreted the process of their conversion in these terms. Similarly, the remarkable circumstance that so many of the greatest capitalistic entrepreneurs — down to Cecil Rhodes — have come from clergymen's families might be explained reaction against their ascetic upbringing. But this form of explanation fails where an extraordinary capitalistic business sense is combined in the same persons and groups with the most intensive forms of a piety which penetrates and dominates their whole lives. Such cases are not isolated, but these traits are characteristic of many of the most important Churches and sects in the history of Protestantism. Especially Calvinism, wherever it has appeared,[4] has shown this combination. However little, in the time of the expansion of the Reformation, it (or any other Protestant belief) was bound up with any particular social class, it is characteristic and in a certain sense typical that in French Huguenot Churches monks and businessmen (merchants, craftsmen) were particularly numerous among the proselytes, especially at the time of the persecution. Even the Spaniards knew that heresy (*i.e.* the Calvinism of the Dutch) promoted trade, and this coincides with the opinions which Sir William Petty expressed in his discussion of the reasons for the capitalistic development of the Netherlands. Gothein rightly calls the Calvinistic diaspora the seedbed of capitalistic economy. Even in this case one might consider the decisive factor to be the superiority of the French and Dutch economic cultures from which these communities sprang, or perhaps the immense influence of exile in the breakdown of traditional relationships.[5] But in France the situation was, as we know from Colbert's struggles, the same even in the seventeenth century. Even Austria, not to speak of other countries, directly imported Protestant craftsmen.

But not all the Protestant denominations seem to have had an equally strong influence in this direction. That of Calvinism, even in Germany, was among the strongest, it seems, and the reformed faith

---

[4] This, of course, was true only when some possibility of capitalistic development in the area in question was present.

[5] That the simple fact of a change of residence is among the most effective means of intensifying labor is thoroughly established (compare footnote 3). The same Polish girl who at home was not to be shaken loose from her traditional laziness by any chance of earning money, however tempting, seems to change her entire nature and become capable of unlimited accomplishment when she is a migratory worker in a foreign country.

more than the others seems to have promoted the development of the spirit of capitalism, in the Wupperthal as well as elsewhere. Much more so than Lutheranism, as comparison both in general and in particular instances, especially in the Wupperthal, seems to prove.[6] For Scotland, Buckle, and among English poets, Keats, have emphasized these same relationships. Even more striking, as it is only necessary to mention, is the connection of a religious way of life with the most intensive development of business acumen among those sects whose otherworldliness is proverbial as their wealth, especially the Quakers and the Mennonites. The part which the former have played in England and North America fell to the latter in Germany and the Netherlands. That in East Prussia Frederick William I tolerated the Mennonites as indispensable to industry, in spite of their absolute refusal to refusal perform military service, is only one of the numerous well-known cases which illustrates the fact, though, considering the character of that monarch, it is one it is one of the most striking. Finally, that this combination of intense piety with just as strong a development of business acumen, was also characteristic of the Pietists, common knowledge.[7]

It is only necessary to think of the Rhine country and of Calw. In this purely introductory discussion it is unnecessary to pile up more examples. For these few already all show one thing: that the spirit of hard work, of progress, or whatever else it might may be called, the awakening of which one is inclined to ascribe to Protestantism, must not be understood, as there is a tendency to do, as joy of living nor in any other sense as connected with the Enlightenment. The old Protestantism of Luther, Calvin, Knox, Voet, had precious little to do with what today is called progress. To whole aspects of modern life which the most extreme religionist would not wish to suppress today, it was directly hostile. If any inner relationship between certain expressions of the old Protestant spirit and modern capitalistic culture is to be found, we must attempt to find it, for

---

[6] In Hamburg, which is almost entirely Lutheran, the only fortune going back to the seventeenth century is that of a well-known Reformed family (kindly called to my attention by Professor A. Wahl).

[7] Naturally this does not mean that official Pietism, like other religious tendencies, did not at a later date, from a patriarchal point of view, oppose certain progressive features of capitalistic development, for instance, the transition from domestic industry to the factory system.

better or worse, not in its alleged more or less materialistic or at least anti-ascetic joy of living, but in its purely religious characteristics. Montesquieu says (*Esprit des Lois*, Book XX, chap. 7) of the English that they "had progressed the farthest of all peoples of the world in three important things: in piety, in commerce, and in freedom." Is it not possible that their commercial superiority and their adaptation to free political institutions are connected in some way with that record of piety which Montesquieu ascribes to them?

A large number of possible relationships, vaguely perceived, occur to us when we put the question in this way. It will now be our task to formulate what occurs to us confusedly as clearly as is possible, considering the inexhaustible diversity to be found in all historical material. But in order to do this it is necessary to leave behind the vague and general concepts with which we have dealt up to this point, and attempt to penetrate into the peculiar characteristics of and the differences between those great worlds of religious thought which have existed historically in the various branches of Christianity.

Before we can proceed to that, however, a few remarks are necessary, first on the peculiarities of the phenomenon of which we are seeking an historical explanation, then concerning the sense in which such an explanation is possible at all within the limits of these investigations.

Chapter II

The Spirit *of* Capitalism

I n the title of this study is used the somewhat pretentious phrase, the spirit of capitalism. What is to be understood by it? The attempt to give anything like a definition of it brings out certain difficulties which are in the very nature of this type of investigation.

If any object can be found to which this term can be applied with any understandable meaning, it can only be an historical individual, *i.e.* a complex of elements associated in historical reality which we unite into a conceptual whole from the standpoint of their cultural significance.

Such an historical concept, however, since it refers in its content to a phenomenon significant for its unique individuality, cannot be defined according to the formula *genus proximunt, differentia specifica*, but it must be gradually put together out of the individual parts which are taken from historical reality to make it up. Thus the final and definitive concept cannot stand at the beginning of the investigation, but must come at the end. We must, in other words, work out in the course of the discussion, as its most important result, the best conceptual formulation of what we here understand by the spirit of capitalism, that is the best from the point of view which interests us here. This point of view (the one of which we shall speak later) is, further, by no means the only possible one from which the historical phenomena we are investigating can be analyzed. Other standpoints would, for this as for every historical phenomenon, yield other characteristics as the essential ones. The result is that it is by no means necessary to understand by the spirit of capitalism only what it will come to mean to us for the purposes of our analysis. This is a necessary result of the nature of historical concepts which attempt for their methodological purposes not to grasp historical reality in abstract general formulae, but in concrete genetic sets of relations which are inevitably of a specifically unique and individual character.

Thus, if we try to determine the object, the analysis and historical explanation of which we are attempting, it cannot be in the form of a conceptual definition, but at least in the beginning only a provisional description of what is here meant by the spirit of capitalism. Such a description is, however, indispensable in order clearly to understand the object of the investigation. For this purpose we turn to a document of that spirit which contains what we are looking for in almost classical purity, and at the game time has the advantage of being free from all direct relationship to religion, being thus for our purposes, free of preconceptions.

"Remember, that time is money. He that can earn ten shillings a day by his labor, and goes abroad, or sits idle one half of that day, though he spends but sixpence during his diversion or idleness, ought not to reckon that the only expense; he has really spent, rather thrown away, five shilling, besides. "Remember, that credit is money. If a man lets his money lie in my hands after it is due, he gives me interest, or so much as I can make of it during that time. This amounts to a considerable sum where a man has good and large credit, and makes good use of it.

"Remember, that money is of the prolific, generating nature. Money can beget money, and its offspring can beget more, and so on. Five shillings turned is six, turned again it is seven and three pence, and so on, till it becomes a hundred pounds. The more there is of it, the more it produces every turning, so that the profits rise quicker and quicker. He that kills a breeding sow, destroys all her offspring to the thousandth generation. He that murders a crown, destroys all that it might have produced, even scores of pounds."

"Remember this saying, *The good paymaster is lord of another man's purse*. He that is known to pay punctually and exactly to the time he, promises, may at any time, and on any occasion, raise all the money his friends can spare. This is sometimes of great use. After industry and frugality, nothing contributes more to the raising of a young man in the world than punctuality and justice in all his dealings; therefore never keep borrowed money an hour beyond the time you promised, lest a disappointment shut up your friend's purse for ever.

"The most trifling actions that affect a man's credit are to be regarded. The sound of your hammer at five in the morning, or eight at night, heard by a creditor, makes him easy six months longer; but if he sees you at a billiard table, or hears your voice at a tavern, when You should be at work, he sends for his money the next day; demands it, before he can receive it, in a lump. It shows, besides, that you are mindful of what you owe; it makes you appear a careful as well as an honest man, and that still increases your credit.

"Beware of thinking all your own that you possess, and of living accordingly. It is a mistake that many people who have credit fall into. To prevent this, keep an exact account for some time both of your expenses and your income. If you take the pains at first to mention particulars, it will have this good effect: you will discover how wonderfully small, trifling expenses mount up to large sums, and will discern what might have been, and may for the future be saved, without occasioning any great inconvenience."

"For six pounds a year you may have the use of one hundred pounds, provided you are a man of known prudence and honesty.

"He that spends a groat[8] a day idly, spends idly above six pounds a year, which is the price for the use of one hundred pounds.

"He that wastes idly a groat's worth of his time per day, one day with another, wastes the privilege of using one hundred pounds each day.

"He that idly loses five shillings' worth of time, loses five shillings, and might as prudently throw five shillings into the sea.

"He that loses five shillings, not only loses that sum, but all the advantage that might be made by turning it in dealing, which by the time that a young man become: old, will amount to a considerable sum of money."[9]

---

[8] One of several coins formerly used in England, Wales, Scotland, Ireland, British Guiana and the British West Indies

[9] *Der Amerikamüde* (Frankfurt, 1835), well known to be an imaginative paraphrase of Lenau's impressions of America. As a work of art the book would today be

It is Benjamin Franklin who preaches to us in these sentences, the same which Ferdinand Kurnberger satirizes in his clever and malicious *Picture of American Culture* as the supposed confession of faith of the Yankee. That it is the spirit of capitalism which here speaks in characteristic fashion, no one will doubt, however little we may wish to claim that everything which could be understood as pertaining to that spirit is Contained in it. Let us pause a moment to consider this passage, the philosophy of which Kurnberger sums up in the words, "They make tallow out of cattle and money out of men." The peculiarity of this philosophy of avarice appears to be the ideal of the honest man of recognized credit, and above all the idea of a duty of the individual toward the increase of his capital, which is assumed as an end in itself. Truly what is here preached is not simply a means of making one's way in the world, but a peculiar ethic. The infraction of its rules is treated not as foolishness but as forgetfulness of duty. That is the essence of the matter. It is not mere business astuteness, that sort of thing is common enough, it is an ethos. This is the quality which interests us.

When Jacob Fugger, in speaking to a business associate who had retired and who wanted to persuade him to do the same, since he had made enough money and should let others have a chance, rejected that as Pusillanimity and answered that "he (Fugger) thought otherwise, he wanted to make money as long as he could",[10] the spirit of his statement is evidently quite different from that of Franklin. What in the former case was an expression of commercial daring and a Personal inclination morally neutral,[11] in the latter

---

somewhat difficult to enjoy, but it is incomparable as a document of the (now long since blurred-over) differences between the German and the American outlook, one may even say of the type of spiritual life which, in spite of everything, has remained common to all Germans, Catholic and Protestant alike, since the German mysticism of the Middle Ages, as against the Puritan capitalistic valuation of action.

[10] Sombart has used this quotation as a motto for his section dealing with the genesis of capitalism

[11] Which quite obviously does not mean either that Jacob Fugger was a morally indifferent or an irreligious man, or that Benjamin Franklin's ethic is completely covered by the above quotations. It scarcely required Brentano's quotations (*Die Anfänge des modernen Kapitalismus*, pp. 150 ff.) to protect this well-known philanthropist from the misunderstanding which Brentano seems to attribute to me. The problem is just the reverse: how could such a philanthropist come to

takes on the character of ethically colored maxim for the conduct of life. The concept spirit of capitalism is here used in this specific sense, it is the spirit of modern capitalism. For that we are here dealing only with Western European and American capitalism is obvious from the way in which the problem was stated. Capitalism existed in China, India, Babylon, in the classic world, and in the Middle Ages. But in all these cases, as we shall see, this particular ethos was lacking.

Now, all Franklin's moral attitudes are colored with utilitarianism. Honesty is useful, because it assures credit; so are punctuality, industry, frugality, and that is the reason they are virtues. A logical deduction from this would be that where, for instance, the appearance of honesty serves the same purpose, that would suffice, and an unnecessary surplus of this virtue would evidently appear to Franklin's eyes an unproductive waste. And as a matter of fact, the story in his autobiography of his conversion to those virtues,[12] or the discussion of the value of a strict maintenance of the appearance of modesty, the assiduous belittlement of one's own deserts in order to gal general recognition later, confirms this impression. According to Franklin, those virtues, like all others, are only in so far virtues as they are actually useful to the individual, and the surrogate of mere appearance always sufficient when it accomplishes the end view. It is a conclusion which is inevitable for strict utilitarianism. The impression of many Germans t the virtues professed by Americanism are pure hypocrisy seems to have been confirmed by this striking case. But in fact the matter is not by any means so simple.

Benjamin Franklin's own character, as it appears in the really unusual candidness of his autobiography, belies that suspicion. The circumstance that he ascribes his recognition of the utility of virtue to a divine revelation which was intended to lead him in the path of

---

write these particular sentences (the especially characteristic form of which Brentano has neglected to reproduce) in the manner of a moralist?

[12] I grew convinced that truth, sincerity, and integrity in dealings between man and man were of the utmost importance to the felicity of life; and I formed written resolutions, which still remain in my journal book to practice them ever while I lived.

righteousness, shows that something more than mere garnishing for purely egocentric motives is involved.

In fact, the *summum bonum* of his ethic, the earning of more and more money, combined with the strict avoidance of all spontaneous enjoyment of life, is above all completely devoid of any eudemonistic, not to say hedonistic, admixture. It is thought of so purely as an end in itself, that from the point of view of the happiness of, or utility to, the single individual, it appears entirely transcendental and absolutely irrational. Man is dominated by the making of money, by acquisition as the ultimate purpose of his life. Economic acquisition is no longer subordinated to man as the means for the satisfaction of his material needs. This reversal of what we should call the natural relationship, so irrational from a naïve point of view, is evidently as definitely a leading principle of capitalism as it is foreign to all peoples not under capitalistic influence. At the same time it expresses a type of feeling which is closely connected with certain religious ideas. If we thus ask, *why* should "money be made out of men", Benjamin Franklin himself, although he was a colorless deist, answers in his autobiography with a quotation from the Bible, which his strict Calvinistic father drummed into him again and again in his youth: "Seest thou a man diligent in his business? He shall stand before kings" (Prov. xxii. 29). The earning of money within the modern economic order is, so long as it is done legally, the result and the expression of virtue and proficiency in a calling; and this virtue and proficiency are, as it is now not difficult to see, the real Alpha and Omega of Franklin's ethic, as expressed in the passages we have quoted, as well as in all his works without exception.

And in truth this peculiar idea, so familiar to us today, but in reality so little a matter of course, of one's duty in a calling, is what is most characteristic of the social ethic of capitalistic culture, and is in a sense the fundamental basis of it. It is an obligation which the individual is supposed to feel and does feel towards the content of his professional activity, no matter in what it consists, in particular no matter whether it appears on the surface as a utilization of his personal powers, or only of his material possessions (as capital).

Of course, this conception has not appeared only under capitalistic conditions. On the contrary, we shall, later trace its origins back to a time previous to the advent of capitalism. Still less, naturally, do we maintain: that a conscious acceptance of these ethical maxims on the part of the individuals, entrepreneurs or laborers in modem capitalistic enterprises, is a condition of the further existence of present day capitalism. The capitalistic economy of the present day is an immense cosmos into which the individual is born, and which presents itself to him, at least as an individual, as an unalterable order of things in which he must live. It forces the individual, in so far as he is involved in the system of market relationships, to conform to capitalistic rules of action. The manufacturer who in the long run acts counter to these norms, will just as inevitably be eliminated from the economic scene as the worker who cannot or will not adapt himself to them will be thrown into the streets without a job.

Thus the capitalism of today, which has come t dominate economic life, educates and selects the economic subjects which it needs through a process of economic survival of the fittest. But here one can easily see the limits of the concept of selection as a means of historical explanation. In order that a manner of life so well adapted to the peculiarities of capitalism could be selected at all, *i.e.* should come to dominate others, it had to originate somewhere, and not in isolated individuals alone, but as a way of life common to whole groups of men. This origin is what really needs explanation. Concerning the doctrine of the more naïve historical materialism, that such ideas originate as a reflection or superstructure of economic situations, we shall speak more in detail below. At this point it will suffice for our purpose to call attention to the fact that without doubt, in the country of Benjamin Franklin's birth (Massachusetts), the spirit of capitalism (in the sense we have attached to it) was present before the capitalistic order. There were complaints of a peculiarly Calculating sort of profit seeking in New England, as distinguished from other parts of America, as early as 1632. It is further undoubted that capitalism remained far less developed in some of the neighboring colonies, the later Southern States of the United States of America, in spite of the fact that these latter were founded by large capitalists for business motives, while the New England colonies were founded by preachers and seminary graduates with the help of small bourgeois, craftsmen and yeomen, for religious reasons. In this case the causal relation is certainly the reverse of that suggested by the materialistic standpoint.

But the origin and history of such ideas is much more complex than the theorists of the superstructure suppose. The spirit of capitalism, in the sense in which we are using the term, had to fight its way to supremacy against a whole world of hostile forces. A state of mind such as that expressed in the passages we have quoted from Franklin, and which called forth the applause of a whole people, would both in ancient times and in the Middle Ages[C] have been proscribed as the lowest sort of avarice and as an attitude entirely lacking in self respect. It is, in fact, still regularly thus looked upon by all those social groups which are least involved in or adapted to modern capitalistic conditions. This is not wholly because the instinct of acquisition was in those times unknown or undeveloped, as has often been said. Nor because the *auri sacra fames*, the greed for gold, was then, or now, less powerful outside of bourgeois capitalism than within its peculiar sphere, as the illusions of modern romanticists are wont to believe. The difference between the capitalistic and pre-capitalistic spirits is not to be found at this point. The greed of the Chinese Mandarin, the old Roman aristocrat, or the modern peasant, can stand up to any comparison. And the *auri sacra fames* of a Neapolitan cab driver or *barcaiuolo*, and certainly of Asiatic representatives of similar trades, as well as of the craftsmen of southern European or Asiatic countries is, as anyone can find out for himself, very much more intense, and especially more unscrupulous than that of, say, an Englishman in similar circumstances.[13]

The universal reign of absolute unscrupulousness in the pursuit of selfish interests by the making of money has been a specific characteristic of precisely those countries whose bourgeois-capitalistic development, measured according to Occidental standards, has remained backward. As every employer knows, the lack of *coscienziosita* of the laborers of such countries, for instance Italy as compared with Germany, has been, and to a certain extent still is, one of the principal obstacles to their capitalistic

---

[13] Unfortunately Brentano (*op. cit.*) has thrown every kind of struggle for gain, whether peaceful or warlike, into one pot, and has then set up as the specific criterion of capitalistic (as contrasted, for instance, with feudal) profit-seeking, its acquisitiveness of *money* (instead of land).

development. Capitalism cannot make use of the labor of those who practice the doctrine of undisciplined *liberumarbitrium*, any more than it can make use of the business man who seems absolutely unscrupulous in his dealings with others, as we can learn from Franklin. Hence the difference does not lie in the degree of development of any impulse to make money. The *auri sacra fames* is as old as the history of man. But we shall see that those who submitted to it without reserve as an uncontrolled impulse, such as the Dutch sea captain who "would go through hell for gain, even though he scorched his sails", were by no means the representatives of that attitude of mind from which the specifically modern capitalistic spirit as a mass phenomenon is derived, and that is what matters. At all periods of history, wherever it was possible, there has been ruthless acquisition, bound to no ethical norms whatever. Like war and piracy, trade has often been unrestrained in its relations with foreigners and those outside the group. The double ethic has permitted here what was forbidden in dealings among brothers.

Capitalistic acquisition as an adventure has been at home in all types of economic society which have known trade with the use of money and which have offered it opportunities, through *commenda*, farming of taxes, State loans, financing of wars, ducal courts and office holders. Likewise the inner attitude of the adventurer, which laughs at all ethical limitations, has been universal. Absolute and conscious ruthlessness in acquisition has often stood in the closest connection with the strictest conformity to tradition. Moreover, with the breakdown of tradition and the more or less complete extension of free economic enterprise, even to within the social group, the new thing has not generally been ethically justified and encouraged, but only tolerated as a fact. And this fact has been treated either as ethically indifferent or as reprehensible, but unfortunately unavoidable. This has not only been the normal attitude of all ethical teachings, but, what is more important, also that expressed in the practical action of the average man of pre-capitalistic times, pre-capitalistic in the sense that the rational utilization of capital in a permanent enterprise and the rational capitalistic organization of labor had not yet become dominant forces in the determination of economic activity. Now just this attitude was one of the strongest inner obstacles which the adaptation of men to the conditions of an ordered bourgeois-capitalistic economy has encountered everywhere.

The most important opponent, with which the spirit of capitalism, in the sense of a definite standard of life claiming ethical sanction, has had to struggle, was that type of attitude and reaction to new situations which we may designate as traditionalism. In this case also every attempt at a final definition must be held in abeyance. On the other hand, lye must try to make the provisional meaning clear by citing a few cases. We will begin from below, with the laborers.

One of the technical means which the modern employer uses in order to secure the greatest possible amount of work from his men is the device of piece rates. In agriculture, for instance, the gathering of the harvest is a case where the greatest possible intensity of labor is called for, since, the weather being uncertain, the difference between high profit and heavy loss may depend on the speed with which the harvesting can be done. Hence a system of piece rates is almost universal in this case. And since the interest of the employer in a speeding. up of harvesting increases with the increase of the results and the intensity of the work, the attempt has again and again been made, by increasing the piece rates of the workmen, thereby giving them an opportunity to earn what is for them a very high wage, to interest them in increasing their own efficiency. But a Peculiar difficulty has been met with surprising frequency: raising the Piece rates has often had the result that not more but less has been accomplished in the same time, because the worker reacted to the increase not by increasing but by decreasing the amount of his work. A man, for instance, who at the rate of 1 mark per acre mowed 2 1/2 acres per day and earned 2 1/2 marks, when the rate was raised to 1.25 marks per acre mowed, not 3 acres, as he might easily have done, thus earning 3.75 marks, but only 2 acres, so that he could still earn the 2 1/2 marks to which he was accustomed. The opportunity of earning more was less attractive than that of working less. He did not ask: how much can I earn in a day if 1 do as much work as possible? but: how much must 1 work in order to cam the wage, 2 1/2 marks, which I earned before and which takes care of my traditional needs? This is an example of what is here meant by traditionalism. A man does not "by nature" wish to cam more and more money, but simply to live as he is accustomed to live and to earn as much as is necessary for that purpose. Wherever modern capitalism has begun its work of increasing the productivity of human labor by increasing its intensity, it has encountered the immensely stubborn resistance of this leading trait of pre-capitalistic labor. And today it encounters it the more, the more backward (from a capitalistic point of view) the laboring forces are with which it has to deal.

Another obvious possibility, to return to our example, since the appeal to the acquisitive instinct through higher wage rates failed, would have been to try the opposite policy, to force the worker by reduction of his wage rates to work harder to cam the same amount than he did before. Low wages and high profits seem even today to a superficial observer to stand in correlation; everything which is paid out in wages seems to involve a corresponding reduction of profits. That road capitalism has taken again and again since its beginning. For centuries it was an article of faith, that low wages were productive, *i.e.* that they increased the material results of labor so that, as Pieter de la Cour, on this point, as we shall see, quite in the spirit of the old Calvinism, said long ago, the people only work because and so long as they are poor.

But the effectiveness of this apparently so efficient method has its limits.[14] Of course the presence of a surplus population which it can hire cheaply in the labor market is a necessity for the development of Capitalism. But though too large a reserve army may in certain cases favor its quantitative expansion, it checks its qualitative development, especially the transition to types of enterprise which make more intensive use of labor. Low wages are by no means identical with cheap labor. From a purely quantitative point of view the efficiency of labor decreases with a wage which is physiologically insufficient, which may in the long run even mean a survival of the unfit. The present day average Silesian mows, when he exerts himself to the full, little more than two thirds as much land as the better paid and nourished Pomeranian or Mecklenburger, and the Pole, the further East he comes from, accomplishes progressively

---

[14] Of course we cannot here enter into the question of where these limits lie, nor can we evaluate the familiar theory of the relation between high wages and the high productivity of labor.

less than the German. Low wages fail even from a purely business point of view wherever it is a question of producing goods which require any sort of skilled labor, or the use of expensive machinery which is easily damaged, or in general wherever any great amount of sharp attention or of initiative is required. Here low wages do not pay, and their effect is the opposite of what was intended. For not only is a developed sense of responsibility absolutely indispensable, but in general also an attitude which, at least during working hours, is freed from continual calculations of how the customary wage May be earned with a maximum of comfort and a minimum of exertion. Labor must, on the contrary, be performed as if it were an absolute end in itself, a calling. But such an attitude is by no means a product of nature. It cannot be evoked by low wages or high ones alone, but can only be the product of a long and arduous process of education. Today, capitalism, once in the saddle, can recruit its laboring force in all industrial countries with comparative ease. In the past this was in every case an extremely difficult problem.[15] And even today it could probably not get along without the support of a powerful ally along the way, which, as we shall see below, was at hand at the time of its development.

What is meant can again best be explained by means of an example. The type of backward traditional form of labor is today very often exemplified by women workers, especially unmarried ones. An almost universal complaint of employers of girls, for instance German girls, is that they are almost entirely unable and unwilling to give up methods of work inherited or once learned in favor of more efficient ones, to adapt themselves to new methods, to learn and to concentrate their intelligence, or even to use it at all. Explanations of the possibility of making work easier, above all more profitable to themselves, generally encounter a complete lack of understanding. Increases of piece rates are without avail against the stone wall of habit. In general it is otherwise, and that is a point of no little importance from our viewpoint, only with girls having a specifically religious, especially a Pietistic, background. One often bears, and statistical investigation confirms it, that by far the best chances of economic education are found among this group. The

---

[15] The establishment even of capitalistic industries has hence often not been possible without large migratory movements from areas of older culture.

ability of mental concentration, as well as the absolutely essential feeling of obligation to one's job, are here most often combined with a strict economy which calculates the possibility of high earnings, and a cool self-control and frugality which enormously increase performance. This provides the most favorable foundation for the conception of labor as an end in itself, as a calling which is necessary to capitalism: the chances of overcoming traditionalism are greatest on account of the religious upbringing. This observation of present-day capitalism[16] in itself suggests that it is worthwhile to ask how this connection of adaptability to capitalism with religious factors may have come about in the days of the early development of capitalism. For that they were even then present in much the same form can be inferred from numerous facts. For instance, the dislike and the persecution which Methodist workmen in the eighteenth century met at the hands of their comrades were not solely nor even principally the result of their religious eccentricities, England had seen many of those and more striking ones. It rested rather, as the destruction of their tools, repeatedly mentioned in the reports, suggests, upon their specific willingness to work as we should say today.

However, let us again return to the present, and this time to the entrepreneur, in order to clarify the meaning of traditionalism in his case.

Sombart, in his discussions of the genesis of capitalism, has distinguished between the satisfaction of needs and acquisition as the two great leading principles in economic history. In the former case the attainment of the goods necessary to meet personal needs, in the latter a struggle for profit free from the limits set by needs, have been the ends controlling the form and direction of economic activity. What he called the economy of needs seems at first glance to be identical with what is here described as economic traditionalism. That may be the case if the concept of needs is

---

[16] The foregoing observations might be misunderstood. The tendency of a well-known type of business man to use the belief that "religion must be maintained for the people" for his own purpose, and the earlier not uncommon willingness of large numbers, especially of the Lutheran clergy, from a general sympathy with authority, to offer themselves as black police when they wished to brand the strike as sin and trade unions as furtherers of cupidity (greed).

limited to traditional needs. But if that is not done, a number of economic types which must be considered capitalistic according to the definition of capital which Sombart gives in another part of his work, would be excluded from the category of acquisitive economy and put into that of needs economy. Enterprises, namely, which are carried on by private entrepreneurs by utilizing capital (money or goods with a money value) to make a profit, purchasing the means of production and selling the product, *i.e.* undoubted capitalistic enterprises, may at the same time have a traditionalistic character. This has, in the course even of modem economic history, not been merely an occasional case, but rather the rule, with continual interruptions from repeated and increasingly powerful conquests of the capitalistic spirit. To be sure the capitalistic form of an enterprise and the spirit in which it is run generally stand in some sort of adequate relationship to each other, but not In one of necessary interdependence. Nevertheless, we provisionally use the expression spirit of (modern) capitalism to describe that attitude which seeks profit rationally and systematically in the manner which we have illustrated, by the example of Benjamin Franklin. This, however, is justified by the historical fact that that attitude of mind has on the one hand found its most suitable expression in capitalistic enterprise, while on the other the enterprise has derived its most suitable motive force from the spirit of capitalism.

But the two may very well occur separately. Benjamin Franklin was filled with the spirit of capitalism at a time when his printing business did not differ in form from any handicraft enterprise. And we shall see that at the beginning of modem times it was by no means the capitalistic entrepreneurs of the commercial aristocracy, who were either the sole or the predominant bearers of the attitude we have here called the spirit of capitalism. It was much more the rising strata of the lower industrial middle classes. Even in the nineteenth century its classical representatives were not the elegant gentlemen of Liverpool and Hamburg, with their commercial fortunes handed down for generations, but the self-made parvenus of Manchester and Westphalia, who often rose from very modest circumstances. As early as the sixteenth century the situation was similar; the industries which arose at that time were mostly created by parvenus.[17]

The management, for instance, of a bank, a wholesale export business, a large retail establishment, or of a large putting-out enterprise dealing with goods produced in homes, is certainly only possible in the form of a capitalistic enterprise. Nevertheless, they may all be carried on in a traditionalistic spirit. In fact, the business of a large bank of issue cannot be carried on in any other way. The foreign trade of whole epochs has rested on the basis of monopolies and legal privileges of strictly traditional character. In retail trade – and we are not here talking of the small men without capital who are continually crying out for Government aid – the revolution which is making an end of the old traditionalism is still in full swing. It is the same development which broke up the old putting-out system, to which modern domestic labor is related only in form. How this revolution takes place and what is its significance may, in spite of the fact these things are so familiar, be again brought out by a concrete example.

Until about the middle of the past century the life of a putter-out was, at least in many of the branches of the Continental textile industry, what we should today consider very comfortable. We may imagine its routine somewhat as follows: The peasants came with their cloth, often (in the case of linen) principally or entirely made from raw material which the peasant himself had produced, to the town in which the putter-out lived, and after a careful, often official, appraisal of the quality, received the customary price for it. The putter-out's customers, for markets any appreciable distance away, were middlemen, who also came to him, generally not yet following samples, but seeking traditional qualities, and bought from his warehouse, or, long before delivery, placed orders which were probably in turn passed on to the peasants. Personal canvassing of customers took place, if at all, only at long intervals. Otherwise correspondence sufficed, though the sending of samples slowly gained ground. The number of business hours was very moderate, perhaps five to six a day, sometimes considerably less; in the rush season, where there was one, more. Earnings were moderate; enough to lead a respectable life and in good times to put away a

---

[17] A person of obscure origin who has gained wealth, influence, or celebrity

little. On the whole, relations among competitors were relatively good, with a large degree of agreement on the fundamentals of business. A long daily visit to the tavern, with often plenty to drink, and a congenial circle of friends, made life comfortable and leisurely.

The form of organization was in every respect capitalistic; the entrepreneur's activity was of a purely business character; the use of capital, turned over in the business, was indispensable; and finally, the objective aspect of the economic process, the bookkeeping, was rational. But it was traditionalistic business, if one considers the spirit which animated the entrepreneur: the traditional manner of life, the traditional rate of profit, the traditional amount of work, the traditional manner of regulating the relationships with labor, and the essentially traditional circle of customers and the manner of attracting new ones. All these dominated the conduct of the business, were at the basis, one may say, of the ethos of this group of business men.

Now at some time this leisureliness was suddenly destroyed, and often entirely without any essential change in the form of organization, such as the transition to a unified factory, to mechanical weaving, etc. What happened was, on the contrary, often no more than this: some young man from one of the putting-out families went out into the country, carefully chose weavers for his employ, greatly increased the rigor of his supervision of their work, and thus turned them from peasants into laborers. On the other hand, he would begin to change his marketing methods by so far as possible going directly to the final consumer, would take the details into his own hands, would personally solicit customers, visiting them every year, and above all would adapt the quality of the product directly to their needs and wishes. At the same time he began to introduce the principle of low prices and large turnover. There was repeated what everywhere and always is the result of such a process of rationalization: those who would not follow suit had to go out of business. The idyllic state collapsed under the pressure of a bitter competitive struggle, respectable fortunes were made, and not lent out at interest, but always reinvested in the business. The old leisurely and comfortable attitude toward life gave way to a hard frugality in which some participated and came to the top, because they did not wish to consume but to earn, while others who wished to keep on with the old ways were forced to curtail their consumption.[18]

And, what is most important in this connection, it was not generally in such cases a stream of new money invested in the industry which brought about this revolution – in several cases known to me the whole revolutionary process was set in motion with a few thousands of capital borrowed from relations – but the new spirit, the spirit of modern capitalism, had set to work. The question of the motive forces in the expansion of modern capitalism is not in the first instance a question of the origin of the capital sums which were available for capitalistic uses, but, above all, of the development of the spirit of capitalism. Where it appears and is able to work itself out, it produces its own capital and monetary supplies as the means to its ends, but the reverse is not true. Its entry on the scene was not generally peaceful. A flood of mistrust, sometimes of hatred, above all of moral indignation, regularly opposed itself to the first innovator. Often – I know of several cases of the sort – regular legends of mysterious shady spots in his previous life have been produced. It is very easy not to recognize that only an unusually strong character could save an entrepreneur of this new type from the loss of his temperate self-control and from both moral and economic shipwreck. Furthermore, along with clarity of vision and ability to it is only by virtue of very definite and highly developed ethical qualities that it has been possible for him to command the absolutely indispensable confidence of his customers and workmen. Nothing else could have given him the strength to overcome the innumerable obstacles, above all the infinitely more intensive work which is demanded of the modern entrepreneur. But these are ethical qualities of quite a different sort from those adapted to the traditionalism of the past.

And, as a rule, it has been neither dare-devil and unscrupulous speculators, economic adventurers such as we meet at all periods of economic history, nor simply great financiers who have carried through this change, outwardly so inconspicuous, but nevertheless

---

[18] For this reason, among others, it is not by chance that this first period of incipient (economic) rationalism in German industry was accompanied by certain other phenomena, for instance the catastrophic degradation of taste in the style of articles of everyday use.

so decisive for the penetration of economic life with the new spirit. On the contrary, they were men who had grown up in the hard school of life, calculating and daring at the same time, above all temperate and reliable, shrewd and completely devoted to their business, with strictly bourgeois opinions and principles. One is tempted to think that these personal moral qualities have not the slightest relation to any ethical maxims, to say nothing of religious ideas, but that the essential relation between them is negative. The ability to free oneself from the common tradition, a sort of liberal enlightenment, seems likely to be the most suitable basis for such a business man's success. And today that is generally precisely the case. Any relationship between religious beliefs and conduct is generally absent, and where any exists, at least in Germany, it tends to be of the negative sort. The people filled with the spirit of capitalism today tend to be indifferent, if not hostile, to the Church. The thought of the pious boredom of paradise has little attraction for their active natures; religion appears to them as a means of drawing people away from labor in this world. If you ask them what is the meaning of their restless activity, why they are never satisfied with what they have, thus appearing so senseless to any purely worldly view of life, they would perhaps give the answer, if they know any at all: "to provide for my children and grandchildren." But more often and, since that motive is not peculiar to them, but was just as effective for the traditionalist, more correctly, simply: that business with its continuous work has become a necessary part of their lives. That is in fact the only possible motivation, but it at the same time expresses what is, seen from the viewpoint of personal happiness, so irrational about this sort of life, where a man exists for the sake of his business, instead of the reverse.

Of course, the desire for the power and recognition which the mere fact of wealth brings plays its part. When the imagination of a whole people has once been turned toward purely quantitative bigness, as in the United States, this romanticism of numbers exercises an irresistible appeal to the poets among business men. Otherwise it is in general not the real leaders, and especially not the permanently successful entrepreneurs, who are taken in by it. In particular, the resort to entailed estates and the nobility, with sons whose conduct at the university and in the officers' corps tries to cover up their social origin, as has been the typical history of German capitalistic parvenu families, is a product of later decadence. The ideal type of the capitalistic entrepreneur, as it has been represented even in Germany by occasional outstanding examples, has no relation to such more or less refined climbers. He avoids ostentation and unnecessary expenditure, as well as conscious enjoyment of his power, and is embarrassed by the outward signs of the social recognition which he receives. His manner of life is, in other words, often, and we shall have to investigate the historical significance of just this important fact, distinguished by a certain ascetic tendency, as appears clearly enough in the sermon of Franklin which we have quoted. It is, namely, by no means exceptional, but rather the rule, for him to have a sort of modesty which is essentially more honest than the reserve which Franklin so shrewdly recommends. He gets nothing out of his wealth for himself, except the irrational sense of having done his job well.

But it is just that which seems to the pre-capitalistic man so incomprehensible and mysterious, so unworthy and contemptible. That anyone should be able to make it the sole purpose of his life-work, to sink into the grave weighed down with a great material load of money and goods, seems to him explicable only as the product of a perverse instinct, the *auri sacra fames*.

At present under our individualistic political, legal, and economic institutions, with the forms of organization and general structure which are peculiar to our economic order, this spirit of capitalism might be understandable, as has been said, purely as a result of adaptation. The capitalistic system so needs this devotion to the calling of making money, it is an attitude toward material goods which is so well suited to that system, so intimately bound up with the conditions of survival in the economic struggle for existence, that there can today no longer be any question of a necessary connection of that acquisitive manner of life with any single *Weltanschauung*. In fact, it no longer needs the support of any religious forces, and feels the attempts of religion to influence economic life, in so far as they can still be felt at all, to be as much an unjustified interference as its regulation by the State. In such circumstances men's commercial and social interests do tend to determine their opinions and attitudes.

Whoever does not adapt his manner of life to the conditions of capitalistic success must go under, or at least cannot rise. But these are phenomena of a time in which modem capitalism has become dominant and has become emancipated from its old supports. But as it could at one time destroy the old forms of medieval regulation of economic life only in alliance with the growing power of the modern State, the same, we may say provisionally, may have been the case in its relations with religious forces. Whether and in what sense that was the case, it is our task to investigate. For that the conception of money-making as an end in itself to which people were bound, as a calling, was contrary to the ethical feelings of whole epochs, it is hardly necessary to prove. The dogma *Deo placere vix potest*[19] which was incorporated into the canon law and applied to the activities of the merchant, and which at that time (like the passage in the gospel about interest)[D] was considered genuine, as well as St. Thomas's characterization of the desire for gain as *turpitudo*[20] (which term even included unavoidable and hence ethically justified profit making), already contained a high degree of concession on the part of the Catholic doctrine to the financial powers with which the Church had such intimate political relations in the Italian cities, as compared with the much more radically anti-chrematistic views of comparatively wide circles. But even where the doctrine was still better accommodated to the facts, as for instance with Anthony of Florence, the feeling was never quite overcome, that activity directed to acquisition for its own sake was at bottom a *pudendum*[21] which was to be tolerated only because of the unalterable necessities of life in this world.

Some moralists of that time, especially of the nominalistic school, accepted developed capitalistic business forms as inevitable, and attempted to justify them, especially commerce, as necessary. The *industria* developed in it they were able to regard, though not without contradictions, as a legitimate source of profit, and hence ethically unobjectionable. But the dominant doctrine rejected the spirit of capitalistic acquisition as *turpitudo*, or at least could not give

---

[19] "He (the merchant) can scarcely please God." *Latin*

[20] Ugliness, deformity; shame - *Latin*

[21] The external genital organs, esp. of a female. From Latin *pudenda* ("that whereof one ought to feel shame")

it a positive ethical sanction. An ethical attitude like that of Benjamin Franklin would have been simply unthinkable. This was, above all, the attitude of capitalistic circles themselves. Their life-work was, so long as they clung to the tradition of the Church, at best something morally indifferent. It was tolerated, but was still, even if only on account of the continual danger of collision with the Church's doctrine on usury, somewhat dangerous to salvation. Quite considerable sums, as the sources show, went at the death of rich people to religious institutions as conscience money, at times even back to former debtors as *usura*[22] which had been unjustly taken from them. It was otherwise, along with heretical and other tendencies looked upon with disapproval, only in those parts of the commercial aristocracy which were already emancipated from the tradition. But even skeptics and people indifferent to the Church often reconciled themselves with it by gifts, because it was a sort of insurance against the uncertainties of what might come after death, or because (at least according to the very widely held latter view) an external obedience to the commands of the Church was sufficient to insure salvation. Here the either non moral or immoral character of their action in the opinion of the participants themselves comes clearly to light.

Now, how could activity, which was at best ethically tolerated, turn into a calling in the sense of Benjamin Franklin? The fact to be explained historically is that in the most highly capitalistic center of that time, in Florence of the fourteenth and fifteenth centuries, the money and capital market of all the great political Powers, this attitude was considered ethically unjustifiable, or at best to be tolerated. But in the backwoods small bourgeois circumstances of Pennsylvania in the eighteenth century, where business threatened for simple lack of money to fall back into barter, where there was hardly a sign of large enterprise, where only the earliest beginnings of banking were to be found, the same thing was considered the essence of moral conduct, even commanded in the name of duty. To speak here of a reflection of material conditions in the ideal superstructure would be patent nonsense. What was the background of ideas which could account for the sort of activity apparently directed toward profit alone as a calling toward which

---

[22] To practice usury; to charge unlawful interest. *Galician.*

the individual feels himself to have an ethical obligation? For it was this idea which gave the way of life of the new entrepreneur its ethical foundation and justification.

The attempt has been made, particularly by Sombart, in what are often judicious and effective observations, to depict economic rationalism as the salient feature of modern economic life as a whole. Undoubtedly with justification, if by that is meant the extension of the productivity of labor which has, through the subordination of the process of production to scientific points of view, relieved it from its dependence upon the natural organic limitations of the human individual. Now this process of rationalization in the field of technique and economic organization undoubtedly determines an important part of the ideals of life of modern bourgeois society. Labor in the service of a rational organization for the provision of humanity with material goods has without doubt always appeared to representatives of the capitalistic spirit as one of the most important purposes of their life-work. It is only necessary, for instance, to read Franklin's account of his efforts in the service of civic improvements in Philadelphia clearly to apprehend this obvious truth. And the joy and pride of having given employment to numerous people, of having had a part in the economic progress of his home town in the sense referring to figures of population and volume of trade which capitalism associated with the word, all these things obviously are part of the specific and undoubtedly idealistic satisfactions in life to modern men of business. Similarly it is one of the fundamental characteristics of an individualistic capitalistic economy that it is rationalized on the basis of rigorous calculation, directed with foresight and caution toward the economic success which is sought in sharp contrast to the hand-to-mouth existence of the peasant, and to the privileged traditionalism of the guild craftsman and of the adventurers' capitalism, oriented to the exploitation of political opportunities and irrational speculation.

It might thus seem that the development of the spirit of capitalism is best understood as part of the development of rationalism as a whole, and could be deduced from the fundamental position of rationalism on the basic problems of life. In the process Protestantism would only have to be considered in so far as it had formed a stage prior to the development of a purely rationalistic philosophy. But any serious attempt to carry this thesis through makes it evident that such a simple way of putting the question will not work, simply because of the fact that the history of rationalism shows a development which by no means follows parallel lines in the various departments of life. The rationalization of private law, for instance, if it is thought of as a logical simplification and rearrangement of the content of the law, was achieved in the highest hitherto known degree in the Roman law of late antiquity. But it remained most backward in some of the countries with the highest degree of economic rationalization, notably in England, where the Renaissance of Roman Law was overcome by the power of the great legal corporations, while it has always retained its supremacy in the Catholic countries of Southern Europe. The worldly rational philosophy of the eighteenth century did not find favor alone or even principally in the countries of highest capitalistic development. The doctrines of Voltaire are even today the common property of broad upper, and what is practically more important, middle class groups in the Romance Catholic countries. Finally, if under practical rationalism is understood the type of attitude which sees and judges the world consciously in terms of the worldly interests of the individual ego, then this view of life was and is the special peculiarity of the peoples of the *liberum arbitrium*,[23] such as the Italians and the French are in very flesh and blood. But we have already convinced ourselves that this is by no means the soil in which that relationship of a man to his calling as a task, which is necessary to capitalism, has preeminently grown. In fact, one may – this simple proposition, which is often forgotten, should be placed at the beginning of every study which essays to deal with rationalism – rationalize life from fundamentally different basic points of view and in very different directions, Rationalism is an historical concept which covers a whole world of different things. It will be our task to find out whose intellectual child the particular concrete form of rational thought was, from which the idea of a calling and the devotion to labor in the calling has grown, which is, as we have seen, so irrational from the standpoint of purely eudemonistic self interest, but which has been and still is one of the most characteristic

---

[23] The ability or discretion to choose; free choice -

elements of our capitalistic culture. We are here particularly interested in the origin of precisely the irrational element which lies in this, as in every conception of a calling.

Chapter III

Luther's Conception *of the* Calling

Task *of the* Investigation

Now it is unmistakable that even in the German word *Beruf,* and perhaps still more clearly in the English calling, a religious conception, that of a task set by God, is at least suggested. The more emphasis is put upon the word in a concrete case, the more evident is the connotation. And if we trace the history of the word through the civilized languages, it appears that neither the predominantly Catholic peoples nor those of classical antiquity[24] have possessed any expression of similar connotation for what we know as a calling (in the sense of a life-task, a definite field in which to work), while one has existed for all predominantly Protestant peoples. It may be further shown that this is not due to any ethnical peculiarity of the languages concerned. It is not, for instance, the product of a Germanic spirit, but in its modern meaning the word comes from the Bible translations, through the spirit of the translator, not that of the original. In Luther's translation of the Bible it appears to have first been used at a point in Jesus Sirach (x i. 20 and 21) precisely in our modern sense. After that it speedily took on its present meaning in the everyday speech of all Protestant peoples, while earlier not even a suggestion of such a meaning could be found in the secular literature of any of them, and even, in religious writings, so far as I can ascertain, it is only found in one of the German mystics whose influence on Luther is well known.

Like the meaning of the word, the idea is new, a product of the Reformation. This may be assumed as generally known. It is true that certain suggestions of the positive valuation of routine activity in the world, which is contained in this conception of the calling, had already existed in the Middle Ages, and even in late Hellenistic

---

[24] Of the ancient languages only Hebrew has any similar concept.

antiquity. We shall speak of that later. But at least one thing was unquestionably new: the valuation of the fulfillment of duty in worldly affairs as the highest form which the moral activity of the individual could assume. This it was which inevitably gave every-day worldly activity a religious significance, and which first created the conception of a calling in this sense. The conception of the calling thus brings out that central dogma of all Protestant denominations which the Catholic division of ethical precepts into *praecepta* and *consilia* discards. The only way of living acceptably to God was not to surpass worldly morality in monastic asceticism, but solely through the fulfillment of the obligations imposed upon the individual by his position in the world. That was his calling.

Luther developed the conception in the course of the first decade of his activity as a reformer. At first, quite in harmony with the prevailing tradition of the Middle Ages, as represented, for example, by Thomas Aquinas he thought of activity in the world as a thing of the flesh, even though willed by God. It is the indispensable natural condition of a life of faith, but in itself, like eating and drinking, morally neutral. But with the development of the conception of *sola fide* in all its consequences, and its logical result, the increasingly sharp emphasis against the Catholic *consilia evangelica* of the monks as dictates of the devil, the calling grew in importance. The monastic life is not only quite devoid of value as a means of justification before God, but he also looks upon its renunciation of the duties of this world as the product of selfishness, withdrawing from temporal obligations. In contrast, labor in a calling appears to him as the outward expression of brotherly love. This he proves by the observation that the division of labor forces every individual to work for others, but his viewpoint is highly naïve, forming an almost grotesque contrast to Adam Smith's well known statements on the same subject.[25] However, this justification, which is evidently essentially scholastic, soon disappears again, and there remains, more and more strongly emphasized, the statement that the fulfillment of worldly duties is under all circumstances the only way

---

[25] "It is not from the benevolence of the butcher, the brewer, or the baker, that we expect our dinner, but from their regard to their own interest. We address ourselves, not to their humanity, but to their self-love; and never talk to them of our own necessities, but of their advantages" (*Wealth of Nations*, Book I, chap. ii).

to live acceptably to God. It and it alone is the will of God, and hence every legitimate calling has exactly the same worth in the sight of God.

That this moral justification of worldly activity was one of the most important results of the Reformation, especially of Luther's part in it, is beyond doubt, and may even be considered a platitude. This attitude is worlds removed from the deep hatred of Pascal, in his contemplative moods, for all worldly activity, which he was deeply convinced could only be understood in terms of vanity or low cunning. And it differs even more from the liberal utilitarian compromise with the world at which the Jesuits arrived. But just what the practical significance of this achievement of Protestantism was in detail is dimly felt rather than clearly perceived.

In the first place it is hardly necessary to point out that Luther cannot be claimed for the spirit of capitalism in the sense in which we have used that term above, or for that matter in any sense whatever. The religious circles which today most enthusiastically celebrate that great achievement of the Reformation are by no means friendly to capitalism in any sense. And Luther himself would, without doubt, have sharply repudiated any connection with a point of view like that of Franklin. Of course, one cannot consider his complaints against the great merchants of his time, such as the Fuggers,[26] as evidence in this case. For the struggle against the privileged position, legal or actual, of single great trading companies in the sixteenth and seventeenth centuries may best be compared with the modem campaign against the trusts, and can no more justly be considered in itself an expression of a traditionalistic point of view. Against these people, against the Lombards, the monopolists, speculators, and bankers patronized by the Anglican Church and the kings and parliaments of England and France, both the Puritans and the Huguenots carried on a bitter struggle. Cromwell, after the battle of Dunbar (September 1650), wrote to the Long Parliament: "Be

---

[26] Apropos of the Fuggers, he thinks that it "cannot be right and godly for such a great and regal fortune to be piled up in the lifetime of one man." That is evidently the peasant's mistrust of capital. Similarly (*Grosser Sermon vom Wucher,* Erlangen edition, XX, p. 109) investment in securities he considers ethically undesirable, because it is *"ein neues behendes erfunden Ding"* —i.e. because it is to him economically incomprehensible; somewhat like margin trading to the modern clergyman.

pleased to reform the abuses of all professions: and if there be any one that makes many poor to make a few rich, that suits not a Commonwealth." But, nevertheless, we will find Cromwell following a quite specifically capitalistic line of thought. On the other hand, Luther's numerous statements against usury or interest in any form reveal a conception of the nature of capitalistic acquisition which, compared with that of late Scholasticism, is, from a capitalistic viewpoint, definitely backward. Especially, of course, the doctrine of the sterility of money which Anthony of Florence had already refuted.

But it is unnecessary to go into detail. For, above all the consequences of the conception of the calling in the religious sense for worldly conduct were susceptible to quite different interpretations. The effect of the Reformation as such was only that, as compared with the Catholic attitude, the moral emphasis on and the religious sanction of, organized worldly labor in a calling was mightily increased. The way in which the concept of the calling, which expressed this change, should develop further depended upon the religious evolution which now took place in the different Protestant Churches. The authority of the Bible, from which Luther thought he had derived his idea of the calling, on the whole favored a traditionalistic interpretation. The Old Testament, in particular, though in the genuine prophets it showed no sign of a tendency to excel worldly morality, and elsewhere only in quite isolated rudiments and suggestions, contained a similar religious idea entirely in this traditionalistic sense. Everyone should abide by his living and let the godless run after gain. That is the sense of all the statements which bear directly on worldly activities. Not until the Talmud is a partially, but not even then fundamentally, different attitude to be found. The personal attitude of Jesus is characterized in classical purity by the typical antique Oriental plea: "Give us this day our daily bread." The element of radical repudiation of the world, as expressed in the (Greek Term), excluded the possibility that the modern idea of calling should be based on his personal authority. In the apostolic era as expressed in the New Testament, especially in St. Paul, the Christian looked upon worldly activity either with indifference, or at least essentially traditionalistically; for those first generations were filled with eschatological hopes. Since everyone was simply waiting for the coming of the Lord, there was nothing to do but remain in the station and in the worldly occupation in which the call of the Lord had found him, and labor as before. Thus he would not burden his brothers as an object of charity, and it would only be for a little while. Luther read the Bible through the spectacles of his whole attitude; at the time and in the course of his development from about 1518 to 1530 this not only remained traditionalistic but became ever more so.[27]

In the first years of his activity as a reformer he was, since he thought of the calling as primarily of the flesh, dominated by an attitude closely related, in so far as the form of world activity was concerned, to the Pauline eschatological indifference as expressed in I Cor. vii. One may attain salvation in any walk of life; on the short pilgrimage of life there is no use in laying weight on the form of occupation. The pursuit of material gain beyond personal needs must thus appear as a symptom of lack of grace, and since it can apparently only be attained at the expense of others, directly reprehensible. As he became increasingly involved in the affairs of the world, he came to value work in the world more highly. But in the concrete calling an individual pursued he saw more and more a special command of God to fulfill these particular duties which the Divine Will had imposed upon him. And after the conflict with the

---

[27] With what follows, compare above all the discussion in Eger, *op. cit.* Also Schneckenburger's fine work, which is even today not yet out of date (*Vergleichende Darstellung der lutherischen und reformierten Lehrbegriffe*, Grüder, Stuttgart, 1855). Luthardt's *Ethik Luthers*, p. 84 of the first edition, the only one to which I have had access, gives no real picture of the development. Further compare Seeberg, *Dogmengeschichte*, II, pp. 262 ff. The article on *Beruf* in the *Realenzyklopädie für protestantische Theologie und Kirche* is valueless. Instead of a scientific analysis of the conception and its origin, it contains all sorts of rather sentimental observations on all possible subjects, such as the position of women, etc. Of the economic literature on Luther, I refer here only to Schmoller's studies ("Geschichte der Nationalökonomischen Ansichten in Deutschland während der Reformationszeit", *Zeitschrift f. Staatswiss.*, XVI, 1860); Wiskemann's prize essay (1861); and the study of Frank G. Ward ("*Darstellung und Würdigung von Luthers Ansichten vom Staat und seinen wirtschaftlichen Aufgaben*", *Conrads Abhandlungen*, XXI, Jena, 1898). The literature on Luther in commemoration of the anniversary of the Reformation, part of which is excellent, has, so far as I can see, made no definite contribution to this particular problem. On the social ethics of Luther (and the Lutherans) compare, of course, the relevant parts of Troeltsch's *Soziallehren*.

Fanatics and the peasant disturbances, the objective historical order of things in which the individual has been placed by God becomes for Luther more and more a direct manifestation of divine will. The stronger and stronger emphasis on the providential element, even in particular events of life, led more and more to a traditionalistic interpretation based on the idea of Providence. The individual should remain once and for all in the station and calling in which God had placed him, and should restrain his worldly activity within the limits imposed by his established station in life. While his economic traditionalism was originally the result of Pauline indifference, it later became that of a more and more intense belief in divine providence, which identified absolute obedience to God's will, with absolute acceptance of things as they were. Starting from this background, it was impossible for Luther to establish a new or in any way fundamental connection between worldly activity and religious principles. His acceptance of purity of doctrine as the one infallible criterion of the Church, which became more and more irrevocable after the struggles of the twenties, was in itself sufficient to check the development of new points of view in ethical matters.

Thus for Luther the concept of the calling remained traditionalistic. His calling is something which man has to accept as a divine ordinance, to which he must adapt himself. This aspect outweighed the other idea which was also present, that work in the calling was a, or rather the, task set by God. And in its further development, orthodox Lutheranism emphasized this aspect still more. Thus, for the time being, the only ethical result was negative; worldly duties were no longer subordinated to ascetic ones; obedience to authority and the acceptance of things as they were, were preached.[28] In this Lutheran form the idea of a calling had, as

---

[28] This explains why, in contrast to what has been said about the effects of Pietism on women workers, modern business men sometimes maintain that strict Lutheran domestic workers today often, for instance in Westphalia, think very largely in traditional terms. Even without going over to the factory system, and in spite of the temptation of higher earnings, they resist changes in methods of work, and in explanation maintain that in the next world such trifles won't matter anyway. It is evident that the mere fact of Church membership and belief is not in itself of essential significance for conduct as a whole. It has been much more concrete religious values and ideals which have influenced the development of capitalism in its early stages and, to a lesser extent, still do.

will be shown in our discussion of medieval religious ethics, to a considerable extent been anticipated by the German mystics. Especially in Tauler's equalization of the values of religious and worldly occupations, and the decline in valuation of the traditional forms of ascetic practices on account of the decisive significance of the ecstatic-contemplative absorption of the divine spirit by the soul. To a certain extent Lutheranism means a step backward from the mystics, in so far as Luther, and still more his Church, had, as compared with the mystics, partly undermined the psychological foundations for a rational ethics. (The mystic attitude on this point is reminiscent partly of the Pietest and partly of the Quaker psychology of faith.) That was precisely because he could not but suspect the tendency to ascetic self discipline of leading to salvation by works, and hence he and his Church were forced to keep it more and more in the background.

Thus the mere idea of the calling in the Lutheran sense is at best of questionable importance for the problems in which we are interested. This was all that was meant to be determined here. But this is not in the least to say that even the Lutheran form of the renewal of the religious life may not have had some practical significance for the objects of our investigation; quite the contrary. Only that significance evidently cannot be derived directly from the attitude of Luther and his Church to worldly activity, and is perhaps not altogether so easily grasped as the connection with other branches of Protestantism. It is thus well for us next to look into those forms in which a relation between practical life and a religious motivation can be more easily perceived than in Lutheranism. We have already called attention to the conspicuous part played by Calvinism and the Protestant sects in the history of capitalistic development. As Luther found a different spirit at work in Zwingli than in himself, so did his spiritual successors in Calvinism. And Catholicism has to the present day looked upon Calvinism as its real opponent.

Now that may be partly explained on purely political grounds. Although the Reformation is unthinkable without Luther's own personal religious development, and was spiritually long influenced by his personality, without Calvinism his work could not have had permanent concrete success. Nevertheless, the reason for this common repugnance of Catholics and Lutherans lies, at least partly, in the ethical peculiarities of Calvinism. A purely superficial glance shows that there is here quite a different relationship between the religious life and earthly activity than in either Catholicism or Lutheranism. Even in literature motivated purely by religious factors that is evident. Take for instance the end of the Divine Comedy, where the poet in Paradise stands speechless in his passive contemplation of the secrets of God, and compare it with the poem which has come to be called the *Divine Comedy* of Puritanism. Milton closes the last song of *Paradise Lost* after describing the expulsion from paradise as follows:

> "They, looking back, all the eastern side beheld
> Of paradise, so late their happy scat,
> Waved over by that flaming brand; the gate
> With dreadful faces thronged and fiery arms.
> Some natural tears they dropped, but wiped them soon:
> The world was all before them, there to choose
> Their place of rest, and Providence their guide."

And only a little before Michael had said to Adam:

> . . . "Only add
> Deeds to thy knowledge answerable; add faith;
> Add virtue, patience, temperance; add love,
> By name to come called Charity, the soul
> Of all the rest: then wilt thou not be loth[29]
> To leave this Paradise, but shall possess
> A Paradise within thee, happier far."

One feels at once that this powerful expression of the Puritan's serious attention to this world, his acceptance of his life in the world as a task, could not possibly have come from the pen of a medieval writer. But it is just as uncongenial to Lutheranism, as expressed for instance in Luther's and Paul Gerhard's chorales. It is now our task to replace this vague feeling by a somewhat more precise logical formulation, and to investigate the fundamental basis of these differences. The appeal to national character is generally a mere confession of ignorance, and in this case it is entirely untenable. To

---

[29] Reluctant; unwilling.

ascribe a unified national character to the Englishmen of the seventeenth century would be simply to falsify history. Cavaliers and Roundheads did not appeal to each other simply as two parties, but a radically distinct species of men, and whoever look into the matter carefully must agree with them. On the other hand, a difference of character between the English merchant adventurers and the old Hanseatic merchants is not to be found; nor can any other fundamental difference between the English and German characters at the end of the Middle Ages, which cannot easily be explained by the differences of their political history.[30] It was the power of religious influence, not alone, but more than anything else, which created the differences of which we are conscious today.

We thus take as our starting-point in the investigation of the relationship between the old Protestant ethic and the spirit of capitalism the works of Calvin, of Calvinism, and the other Puritan sects. But it is not to be understood that we expect to find any of the founders or representatives of these religious movements considering the promotion of what we have called the spirit of capitalism as in any sense the end of his life-work. We cannot well maintain that the pursuit of worldly goods, conceived as a n end in itself, was to any of them of positive ethical value. Once and for all it must be remembered that programs of ethical reform never were at the center of interest for any of the religious reformers (among whom, for our purposes, we must include men like Menno, George Fox, and Wesley). They were not the founders of societies for ethical culture nor the proponents of humanitarian projects for social reform or cultural ideals. The salvation of the soul and that alone was the center of their life and work. Their ethical ideals and the practical results of their doctrines were all based on that alone, and were the consequences of purely religious motives. We shall thus have to admit that the cultural consequences of the Reformation were to a great extent, perhaps in the particular aspects with which we are dealing predominantly, unforeseen and even unwished for results of the labors of the reformers. They were often far removed

---

[30] Especially the English national pride, a result of Magna Charta and the great wars. The saying, so typical today, "She looks like an English girl" on seeing any pretty foreign girl, is reported as early as the 15th century.

from or even in contradiction to all that they themselves thought to attain.

The following study may thus perhaps in a modest way form a contribution to the understanding of the manner in which ideas become effective forces in history. In order, however, to avoid any misunderstanding of the sense in which any such effectiveness of purely ideal motives is claimed at all, I may perhaps be permitted a few remarks in conclusion to this introductory discussion.

In such a study, it may at once be definitely stated, no attempt is made to evaluate the ideas of the Reformation in any sense, whether it concern their social or their religious worth. We have continually to deal with aspects of the Reformation which must appear to the truly religious consciousness as incidental and even superficial. For we are merely attempting to clarify the part which religious forces have played in forming the developing web of our specifically worldly modern culture, in the complex interaction of innumerable different historical factors. We are thus inquiring only to what extent certain characteristic features of this culture can be imputed to the influence of the Reformation. At the same time we must free ourselves from the idea that it is possible to deduce the Reformation, as a historically necessary result, from certain economic changes. Countless historical circumstances, which cannot be reduced to any economic law, and are not susceptible of economic explanation of any sort, especially purely political processes, had to concur in order that the newly created Churches should survive at all.

On the other hand, however, we have no intention whatever of maintaining such a foolish and doctrinaire thesis[31] as that the spirit of capitalism (in the provisional sense of the term explained above) could only have arisen as the result of certain effects of the Reformation, or even that capitalism as an economic system is a creation of the Reformation. In itself, the fact that certain important forms of capitalistic business organization are known to be considerably older than the Reformation is a sufficient refutation of such a claim On the contrary, we only wish to ascertain whether and to what extent religious forces have taken part in qualitative

---

[31] In spite of this and the following remarks, which in my opinion are clear enough, and have never been changed, I have again and again been accused of this.

formation and the quantitative expansion of that spirit over the world. Furthermore, what concrete aspects of our capitalistic culture can be traced to them, In view of the tremendous confusion of interdependent influences between the material basis, the forms of social and political organization, and the ideas current in the time of the Reformation, we can only proceed by investigating whether and at what points certain correlations between forms of religious belief and practical ethics can be worked out. At the same time we shall as far as possible clarify the manner and the general *direction* in which, by virtue of those relationships, the religious movements have influenced the development of material culture. Only when this has been determined with reasonable accuracy can the attempt be made to estimate to what extent the historical development of modern culture can be attributed to those religious forces and to what extent to others.

The Practical Ethics *of the* Ascetic Branches *of* Protestantism

Chapter IV

The Religious Foundations *of* Worldly Asceticism

I n history there have been four principal forms of ascetic Protestantism (in the sense of word here used): (1) Calvinism in the form which it assumed in the main area of its influence in Western Europe, especially in the seventeenth century; (2) Pietism; (3) Methodism; (4) the sects growing out of the Baptist movement. None of these movements was completely separated from the others, and even the distinction from the non-ascetic Churches of the Reformation is never perfectly clear. Methodism, which first arose in the middle of the eighteenth century within the Established Church of England, was not, in the minds of its founders, intended to form a new Church, but only a new awakening of the ascetic spirit within the old. Only in the course of its development, especially in its extension to America, did it become separate from the Anglican Church.

Pietism first split off from the Calvinistic movement in England, and especially in Holland. It remained loosely connected with orthodoxy, shading off from it by imperceptible gradations, until at the end of the seventeenth century it was absorbed into Lutheranism under Spener's leadership. Though the dogmatic adjustment was not entirely satisfactory, it remained a movement within the Lutheran Church. Only the faction dominated by Zinzendorf, and affected by lingering Hussite and Calvinistic influences within the Moravian brotherhood, was forced, like Methodism against its will, to form a peculiar sort of sect. Calvinism and Baptism were at the beginning of their development sharply opposed to each other. But in the Baptism of the latter part of the seventeenth century they were in close contact. And, even in the Independent sects of England and Holland at the beginning of the seventeenth century the transition was not abrupt. As Pietism shows, the transition to Lutheranism is also gradual, and the same is true of Calvinism and the Anglican Church, though both in external character and in the spirit of its most logical adherents the latter is more closely related to Catholicism. It is true that both the mass of the adherents and especially the staunchest champions of that ascetic movement which, in the broadest sense of a highly ambiguous word, has been called Puritanism,[32] did attack the foundations of Anglicanism; but even here the differences were only gradually worked out in the course of the struggle. Even if for the present we quite ignore the questions, of government and organization which do not interest us here, the facts are just the same. The dogmatic differences, even the most important, such as those over the doctrines of predestination and justification, were combined in the most complex ways, and even at the beginning of the seventeenth century regularly, though not without exception, prevented the maintenance of unity in the Church. Above all, the types of moral conduct in which we are interested may be found in similar manner among the adherents of the most various denominations, derived from any one of the four sources mentioned above, or a combination of several of them. We shall see that similar ethical maxims may be correlated with very different dogmatic foundations. Also the important literary tools for the saving of souls, above all the casuistic compendia of the various denominations, influenced each other in the course of time; one finds great similarities in them, in spite of very great differences in actual conduct.

It would almost seem as though we had best completely ignore both the dogmatic foundations and the ethical theory and confine our attention to the moral practice so far as it can be determined.

---

[32] On the development of the concept of Puritanism see, above all, Sanford, *Studies and Reflections of the Great Rebellion*, p. 65 f. When we use the expression it is always in the sense which it took on in the popular speech of the seventeenth century, to mean the ascetically inclined religious movements in Holland and England without distinction of Church organization or dogma, thus including Independents, Congregationalists, Baptists, Mennonites, and Quakers.

That, however, is not true. The various different dogmatic roots of ascetic morality did no doubt die out after terrible struggles. But the original connection with those dogmas has left behind important traces in the later undogmatic ethics; moreover, only the knowledge of the original body of ideas can help us to understand the connection of that morality with the idea of the after-life which absolutely dominated the most spiritual men of that time. Without its power, overshadowing everything else, no moral awakening which seriously influenced practical life came into being in that period.

We are naturally not concerned with the question of what was theoretically and officially taught in the ethical compendia of the time, however much practical significance this may have had through the influence of Church discipline, pastoral work, and preaching. We are interested rather in something entirely different: the influence of those psychological sanctions which, originating in religious belief and the practice of religion, gave a direction to practical conduct and held the individual to it. Now these sanctions were to a large extent derived from the peculiarities of the religious ideas behind them. The men of that day were occupied with abstract dogmas to an extent which itself can only be understood when we perceive the connection of these dogmas with practical religious interests. A few observations on dogma, which will seem to the non-theological reader as dull as they will hasty and superficial to the theologian, are indispensable. We can of course only proceed by presenting these religious ideas in the artificial simplicity of ideal types, as they could at best but seldom be found in history. For just because of the impossibility of drawing sharp boundaries in historical reality we can only hope to understand their specific importance from an investigation of them in their most consistent and logical forms.

A. CALVINISM

Now Calvinism was the faith[33] over which the great political and cultural struggles of the sixteenth and seventeenth centuries were fought in the most highly developed countries, the Netherlands, England, and France. To it we shall hence turn first. At that time, and in general even today, the doctrine of predestination was considered its most characteristic dogma. It is true that there has been controversy as to whether it is the most essential dogma of the Reformed Church or only an appendage. Judgments of the importance of a historical phenomenon may be judgments of value or faith, namely, when they refer to what is. alone interesting, or alone in the long run valuable in it. Or, on the other hand, they may refer to its influence on other historical processes as a causal factor. Then we are concerned with judgments of historical imputation. If now we start, as we must do here, from the latter standpoint and inquire into the significance which is to be attributed to that dogma by virtue of its cultural and historical consequences, it must certainly be rated very highly. The movement which Oldenbameveld led was shattered by it. The schism in the English Church became irrevocable under James I after the Crown and the Puritans came to differ dogmatically over just this doctrine. Again and again it was looked upon as the real element of political danger in Calvinism and attacked as such by those in authority.[34] The great synods of the seventeenth century, above all those of Dordrecht and Westminster, besides numerous smaller ones, made its elevation to canonical authority the central purpose of their work. It served as a rallying point to countless heroes of the Church militant, and in both the eighteenth and the nineteenth centuries it caused schisms in the

---

[33] In the following discussion we are not primarily interested in the origin, antecedents, or history of these ascetic movements, but take their doctrines as given in a state of full development.

[34] Even the Declaration agreed upon between the University of Cambridge and the Archbishop of Canterbury on the 17th Article of the Anglican Confession, the so-called Lambeth Article of 1595, which (contrary to the official version) expressly held that there was also predestination to eternal death, was not ratified by the Queen. The Radicals (as in *Hanserd Knolly's Confession*) laid special emphasis on the express predestination to death (not only the admission of damnation, as the milder doctrine would have it).

Church and formed the battle cry of great new awakenings. We cannot pass it by, and since today it can no longer be assumed as known to all educated men, we can best learn its content from the authoritative words of the Westminster Confession of 1647, which in this regard is simply repeated by both Independent and Baptist creeds.

"Chapter IX (of Free Will), No. 3. Man, by his fall into a state of sin, hath wholly lost all ability of will to any spiritual good accompanying salvation. So that a natural man, being altogether averse from that Good, and dead in sin, is not able, by his own strength, to convert himself, or to prepare himself thereunto.

"Chapter III (of God's Eternal Decree), No. 3. By the decree of God, for the manifestation of His glory, some men and angels are predestinated unto ever-lasting life, and others foreordained to everlasting death.

"No. 5. Those of mankind that are predestinated unto life, God before the foundation of the world was laid, according to His eternal and immutable purpose, and the secret counsel and good pleasure of His will, hath chosen in Christ unto everlasting glory, out of His mere free grace and love, without any foresight of faith or good works, or perseverance in either of them, or any other thing in the creature as conditions, or causes moving Him thereunto, and all to the praise of His glorious grace.

"No. 7. The rest of mankind God was pleased, according to the unsearchable counsel of His own will, whereby He extendeth, or withholdeth mercy, as He pleaseth, for the glory of His sovereign power over His creatures, to pass by, and to ordain them to dishonor and wrath for their sin, to the praise of His glorious justice.

"Chapter X (of Effectual Calling), No. 1. All those whom God hath predestinated unto life, and those only, He is pleased in His appointed and accepted time effectually to call, by His word and spirit (out of that state of sin and death, in which they are by nature) . . . taking away their heart of stone, and giving unto them an heart of flesh; renewing their wills, and by His almighty power determining them to that which is good...

"Chapter V (of Providence), No. 6. As for those wicked and ungodly men, whom God as a righteous judge, for former sins doth blind and harden, from them He not only with-holdeth His grace, whereby they might have been enlightened in their understandings and wrought upon in their hearts, but sometimes also withdraweth the gifts which they had and exposeth them to such objects as their corruption makes occasion of sin: and withal, gives them over to their own lusts, the temptations of the world, and the power of Satan: whereby it comes to pass that they harden themselves, even under those means, which God useth for the softening of others."

"Though I may be sent to Hell for it, such a God will never command my respect", was Milton's well known opinion of the doctrine. But we are here concerned not with the evaluation, but the historical significance of the dogma. We can only briefly sketch the question of how the doctrine originated and how it fitted into the framework of Calvinistic theology.

Two paths leading to it were possible. The phenomenon of the religious sense of grace is combined, in the most active and passionate of those great worshippers which Christianity has produced again and again since Augustine, with the feeling of certainty that that grace is the sole product of an objective power, and not in the least to be attributed to personal worth. The powerful feeling of light-hearted assurance, in which the tremendous pressure of their sense of sin is released, apparently breaks over them with elemental force and destroys every possibility of the belief that this overpowering gift of grace could owe anything to their own cooperation or could be connected with achievements or qualities of their own faith and will. At the time of Luther's greatest religious creativeness, when he was capable of writing his *Freiheit eines Christenmenschen*, God's secret decree was also to him most definitely the sole and ultimate source of his state of religious grace.[35] Even later he did not formally abandon it. But not only did the idea not assume a central position for him, but it receded more and more into the background, the more his position as responsible head of his Church forced him into practical politics. Melancthon quite deliberately avoided adopting the dark and dangerous teaching in the Augsburg Confession, and for the Church fathers of Lutheranism it was an article of faith that grace was revocable

---

[35] *Hic est fides summus gradus; credere Deum esse clementum, qui tam paucos salvat, justum, qui sua voluntate nos damna-biles facit"*, is the text of the famous passage in *De servo arbitrio.*

(*amissibilis*), and could be won again by penitent humility and faithful trust in the word of God and in the sacraments.

With Calvin the process was just the opposite; the significance of the doctrine for him increased,[36] perceptibly in the course of his polemical controversies with theological opponents. It is not fully developed until the third edition of his *Institutes*, and only gained its position of central prominence after his death in the great struggles which the Synods of Dordrecht and Westminster sought to put an end to. With Calvin the *decretum horribile* is derived not, as with Luther, from religious experience, but from the logical necessity of his thought; therefore its importance increases with every increase in the logical consistency of that religious thought. The interest of it is solely in God, not in man; God does not exist for men, but men for the sake of God. All creation, including of course the fact, as it undoubtedly was for Calvin, that only a small pro-portion of men are chosen for eternal grace, can have any meaning only as means to the glory and majesty of God. To apply earthly standards of justice to His sovereign decrees is meaningless and an insult to His Majesty, since He and He alone is free, *i.e.* is subject to no law. His decrees can only be understood by or even known to us in so far as it has been His pleasure to reveal them. We can only hold to these fragments of eternal truth. Everything else, including the meaning of our individual destiny, is hidden in dark mystery which it would be both impossible to pierce and pre-sumptuous to question.

For the damned to complain of their lot would be much the same as for animals to bemoan the fact they were not born as men. For everything of the flesh is separated from God by an unbridgeable gulf and deserves of Him only eternal death, in so far as He has not decreed otherwise for the glorification of His Majesty. We know

---

[36] The truth is that both Luther and Calvin believed fundamentally in a double God (see Ritschl's remarks in *Geschichte des Pietismus* and Köstlin, *Gott in Realenzyklopädie für protestantische Theologie und Kirche*, third edition), the gracious and kindly Father of the New Testament, who dominates the first books of the *Institutio Christiana*, and behind him the *Deus absconditus* as an arbitrary despot. For Luther, the God of the New Testament kept the upper hand, because he avoided reflection on metaphysical questions as useless and dangerous, while for Calvin the idea of a transcendental God won out. In the popular development of Calvinism, it is true, this idea could not be maintained, but what took his place was not the Heavenly Father of the New Testament but the Jehovah of the Old.

only that a part of humanity is saved, the rest damned. To assume that human merit or guilt play a part in determining this destiny would be to think of God's absolutely free decrees, which have been settled from eternity, as subject to change by human influence, an impossible contradiction. The Father in heaven of the New Testament, so human and understanding, who rejoices over the repentance of a sinner as a woman over the lost piece of silver she has found, is gone. His place has been taken by a transcendental being, beyond the reach of human understanding, who with His quite incomprehensible decrees has decided the fate of every individual and regulated the tiniest details of the cosmos from eternity. God's grace is, since His decrees cannot change, as impossible for those to whom He has granted it to lose as it is unattainable for those to whom He has denied it.

In its extreme inhumanity this doctrine must above all have had one consequence for the life of a generation which surrendered to its magnificent consistency. That was a feeling of unprecedented inner loneliness of the single individual.[37] In what was for the man of the age of the Reformation the most important thing in life, his eternal salvation, he was forced to follow his path alone to meet a destiny which had been decreed for him from eternity. No one could help him. No priest, for the chosen one can understand the word of God only in his own heart. No sacraments, for though the sacraments had been ordained by God for the increase of His glory, and must hence be scrupulously observed, they are not a means to the attainment of grace, but only the subjective *externa subsidia* of faith. No Church, for though it was held that extra *ecclesiam nulla salus* in the sense that whoever kept away from the true Church could never belong to God's chosen band, nevertheless the membership of the external Church included the doomed. They should belong to it and be subjected to its discipline, not in order thus to attain salvation, that is impossible, but because, for the glory of God, they too must be forced to obey His commandments. Finally, even no God. For

---

[37] "The deepest community (with God) is found not in institutions or corporations or churches, but in the secrets of a solitary heart", as Dowden puts the essential point in his fine book *Puritan and Anglican* (p. 234).

even Christ had died only for the elect,[38] for whose benefit God had decreed His martyrdom from eternity. This, the complete elimination of salvation through the Church and the sacraments (which was in Lutheranism by no means developed to its final conclusions), was what formed the absolutely decisive difference from Catholicism.

That great historic process in the development of religions, the elimination of magic from the world which had begun with the old Hebrew prophets and, in conjunction with Hellenistic scientific thought, had repudiated all magical means to salvation as superstition and sin, came here to its logical conclusion. The genuine Puritan even rejected all signs of religious ceremony at the grave and buried his nearest and dearest without song or ritual in order that no superstition, no trust in the effects of magical and sacramental forces on salvation, should creep in.[39]

There was not only no magical means of attaining the grace of God for those to whom God had decided to deny it, but no means whatever. Combined with the harsh doctrines of the absolute transcendentiality of God and the corruption of everything pertaining to the flesh, this inner isolation of the individual contains, on the one hand, the reason for the entirely negative attitude of Puritanism to all the sensuous and emotional elements in culture and in religion, because they are of no use toward salvation and promote sentimental illusions and idolatrous superstitions. Thus it provides a basis for a fundamental antagonism to sensuous culture of all kinds.[40] On the other hand, it forms one of the roots of that

---

[38] "It is said that God sent His Son to save the human race, but that was not His purpose, He only wished to help a few out of their degradation—and I say unto you that God died only for the select" (sermon held in 1609 at Broek, near Rogge, Wtenbogaert, II, p. 9. Compare Nuyens, *op. cit.*, II, p. 232).

[39] Similarly the most consistent doctrine held that baptism was required by positive ordinance, but was not necessary to salvation. For that reason the strictly Puritan Scotch and English Independents were able to maintain the principle that children of obvious reprobates should not be baptized (for instance, children of drunkards). An adult who desired to be baptized, but was not yet ripe for the communion, the Synod of Edam of 1586 (Art. 32, 1) recommended should be baptized only if his conduct were blameless, and he should have placed his desires *sonder superstitie*.

[40] This negative attitude toward all sensuous culture is, as Dowden, *op. cit.*, shows, a very fundamental element of Puritanism.

disillusioned and pessimistically inclined individualism[41] which can even today be identified in the national characters and the institutions of the peoples with a Puritan past, in such a striking contrast to the quite different spectacles through which the Enlightenment later looked upon men. We can clearly identify the traces of the influence of the doctrine of predestination in the elementary forms of conduct and attitude toward life in the era with which we are concerned, even where its authority as a dogma was on the decline. It was in fact only the most extreme form of that exclusive trust in God in which we are here interested. It comes out for instance in the strikingly frequent repetition, especially in the English Puritan literature, of warnings against any trust in the aid of friendship of men. Even the amiable Baxter counsels deep distrust of even one's closest friend, and Bailey directly exhorts to trust no one and to say nothing compromising to anyone. Only God should be your confidant. In striking contrast to Lutheranism, this attitude toward life was also connected with the quiet disappearance of the private confession, of which Calvin was suspicious only on account of its possible sacramental misinterpretation, from all the regions of fully developed Calvinism. That was an occurrence of the greatest importance. In the first place it is a symptom of the type of influence this religion exercised. Further, however, it was a psychological stimulus to the development of their ethical attitude. The means to a periodical discharge of the emotional sense of sin was done away with.

Of the consequences for the ethical conduct of everyday life we speak later. But for the general religious situation of a man the consequences are evident. In spite of the necessity of membership in the true Church[42] for salvation, the Calvinist's intercourse with his God was carried on in deep spiritual isolation. To see the specific results of this peculiar atmosphere, it is only necessary to read

---

[41] The expression individualism includes the most heterogeneous things imaginable. What is here understood by it will, I hope, be clear from the following discussion. In another sense of the word, Lutheranism has been called individualistic, because it does not attempt any ascetic regulation of life.

[42] This is a fact which is of special importance for the interpretation of the psychological basis of Calvinistic social organizations. They all rest on spiritually individualistic, rational motives. The individual never enters emotionally into them.

Bunyan's, *Pilgrim's Progress*, by far the most widely read book of the whole Puritan literature. In the description of Christian's attitude after he had realized that he was living in the City of Destruction and he had received the call to take up his pilgrimage to the celestial city, wife and children cling to him, but stopping his ears with his fingers and crying, "life, eternal life", he staggers forth across the fields. No refinement could surpass the naïve feeling of the tinker who, writing in his prison cell, earned the applause of a believing world, in expressing the emotions of the faithful Puritan, thinking only of his own salvation. It is expressed in the unctuous conversations which he holds with fellow-seekers on the way, in a manner somewhat reminiscent of Gottfried Keller's *Gerechte Kammacher*. Only when he himself is safe does it occur to him that it would be nice to have his family with him. It is the same anxious fear of death and the beyond which we feel so vividly in Alfonso of Liguori, as Dollinger has described him to us. It is worlds removed from that spirit of proud worldliness which Machiavelli expresses in relating the fame of those Florentine citizens who, in their struggle against the Pope and his excommunication, had held "Love of their native city higher than the fear for the salvation of their souls." And it is of course even farther from the feelings which Richard Wagner puts into the mouth of Siegmund before his fatal combat, "*Grüsse mir Wotan, grüsse mir Wallhall – Doch von Wallhall's spröden Wonnen sprich du wahrlich mir nicht.*" But the effects of this fear on Bunyan and Liguori are characteristically different. The same fear which drives the latter to every conceivable self humiliation spurs the former on to a restless and systematic struggle with life. Whence comes this difference?

It seems at first a mystery how the undoubted superiority of Calvinism in social organization can be connected with this tendency to tear the individual away from the closed ties with which he is bound to this world.[43] But, however strange it may seem, it follows from the peculiar form which the Christian brotherly love was forced to take under the pressure of the inner isolation of the

---

[43] The Calvinist was fascinated by the idea that God in creating the world, including the order of society, must have willed things to be objectively purposeful as a means of adding to His glory; not the flesh for its own sake, but the organization of the things of the flesh under His will.

individual through the Calvinistic faith. In the first place it follows dogmatically.[44] The world exists to serve the glorification of God and for that purpose alone. The elected Christian is in the world only to increase this glory of God by fulfilling His commandments to the best of his ability. But God requires social achievement of the Christian because He wills that social life shall be organized according to His commandments, in accordance with that purpose. The social activity of the Christian in the world is solely activity in *majorem gloriam Dei*. This character is hence shared by labor in a calling which serves the mundane life of the community. Even in Luther we found specialized labor in callings justified in terms of brotherly love. But what for him remained an uncertain, purely intellectual suggestion became for the Calvinists a characteristic element in their ethical system. Brotherly love, since it may only be practiced for the glory of God[45] and not in the service of the flesh, is expressed in the first place in the fulfillment of the daily tasks given by the *lex naturae*; and in the Process this fulfillment assumes a peculiarly objective and impersonal character, that of service in the interest of the rational organization of our social environment. For the wonderfully purposeful organization and arrangement of this cosmos is, according both to the revelation of the Bible and to natural intuition, evidently designed by God to serve the utility of the human race. This makes labor in the service of impersonal social usefulness appear to promote the glory of God and hence to he willed by Him. The complete elimination of the theodicy problem and of all those questions about the meaning of the world and of life, which have tortured others, was as self-evident to the Puritan as, for quite different reasons, to the Jew, and even in a certain sense to all the non mystical types of Christian religion.

To this economy of forces Calvinism added another tendency which worked in the same direction. The conflict between the individual and the ethic (in Sören Kierkegaard's sense) did not exist for Calvinism, although it placed the individual entirely on his own responsibility in religious matters. This is not the place to analyze

---

[44] Of the relation between dogmatic and practical psychological consequence, the two are not identical.

[45] "Good works performed for any other purpose than the glory of God are sinful." (*Hanserd Knolly's Confession*, chap. xvi).

the reasons for this fact, or its significance for the political and economic rationalism of Calvinism. The source of the utilitarian character of Calvinistic ethics lies here, and important peculiarities of the Calvinistic idea of the calling were derived from the same source as well. But for the moment we must return to the special consideration of the doctrine of predestination.

For us the decisive problem is: How was this doctrine borne in an age to which the after-life was not only more important, but in many ways also more certain, than all the interests of life in this world?[46] The question, Am I one of the elect? must sooner or later have arisen for every believer and have forced all other interests into the background. And how can I be sure of this state of grace?[47] For Calvin himself this was not a problem. He felt himself to be a chosen agent of the Lord, and was certain of his own salvation. Accordingly, to the question of how the individual can be certain of his own election, he has at bottom only the answer that we should be content with the knowledge that God has chosen and depend further only on that implicit trust in Christ which is the result of true faith. He rejects in principle the assumption that one can learn from the conduct of others whether they are chosen or damned. It is an unjustifiable attempt to force God's secrets. The elect differ externally in this life in no way from the damned; and even all the subjective experiences of the chosen are, as *ludibria spiritus sancti*, possible for the damned with the single exception of that *finaliter expectant*, trusting faith. The elect thus are and remain God's invisible Church.

Quite naturally this attitude was impossible for his followers as early as Beza, and, above all, for the broad mass of ordinary men. For them the *certitudo salutis* in the sense of the recognizability of the state of grace necessarily became of absolutely dominant importance. So, wherever the doctrine of predestination was held, the question could not be suppressed whether there were any

---

[46] As is true in such a striking way of the basic atmosphere of Bunyan's *Pilgrim's Progress*.

[47] This question meant less to the later Lutheran, even apart from the doctrine of predestination, than to the Calvinist. Not because he was less interested in the salvation of his soul, but because, in the form which the Lutheran Church had taken, its character as an institution for salvation (*Heilsanstalt*) came to the fore.

infallible criteria by which membership in the *electi* could be known. Not only has this question continually had a central importance in the development of the Pietism which first arose on the basis of the Reformed Church; it has in fact in a certain sense at times been fundamental to it. But when we consider the great political and social importance of the Reformed doctrine and practice of the Communion, we shall see how great a part was played during the whole seventeenth century outside of Pietism by the possibility of ascertaining the state of grace of the individual. On it depended, for instance, his admission to Communion, *i.e.* to the central religious ceremony which determined the social standing of the participants.

It was impossible, at least so far as the question of a man's own state of grace arose, to be satisfied with Calvin's trust in the testimony of the expectant faith resulting from grace, even though the orthodox doctrine had never formally abandoned that criterion." Above all, practical pastoral work, which had immediately to deal with all the suffering caused by the doctrine, could not be satisfied. It met these difficulties in various ways. So far as predestination was not reinterpreted, toned down, or fundamentally abandoned, two principal, mutually connected, types of pastoral advice appear. On the one hand it is held to be an absolute duty to consider oneself chosen, and to combat all doubts as temptations of the devil, since lack of self-confidence is the result of insufficient faith, hence of imperfect grace. The exhortation of the apostle to make fast one's own call is here interpreted as a duty to attain certainty of one's own election and justification in the daily struggle of life. In the place of the humble sinners to whom Luther promises grace if they trust themselves to God in penitent faith are bred those self-confident saints whom we can rediscover in the hard Puritan merchants of the heroic age of capitalism and in isolated instances down to the present. On the other hand, in order to attain that self-confidence intense worldly activity is recommended as the most suitable means. It and it alone disperses religious doubts and gives the certainty of grace.

That worldly activity should be considered capable of this achievement, that it could, so to speak, be considered the most suitable means of counteracting feelings of religious anxiety, finds its explanation in the fundamental peculiarities of religious feeling in the Reformed Church, which come most clearly to light in its differences from Lutheranism in the doctrine of justification by faith. These differences are analyzed so subtly and with such objectivity and avoidance of value judgments in Schneckenburger's excellent lectures, that the following brief observations can for the most part simply rest upon his discussion.

The highest religious experience which the Lutheran faith strives to attain, especially as it developed in the course of the seventeenth century, is the *unio mystica* with the deity.[48] As the name itself, which is unknown to the Reformed faith in this form, suggests, it is a feeling of actual absorption in the deity, that of a real entrance of the divine into the soul of the believer. It is qualitatively similar to the aim of the contemplation of the German mystics and is characterized by its passive search for the fulfillment of the yearning for rest in God.

Now the history of philosophy shows that religious belief which is primarily mystical may very well be compatible with a pronounced sense of reality in the field of empirical fact; it may even support it directly on account of the repudiation of dialectic doctrines. Furthermore, mysticism may indirectly even further the interests of rational conduct. Nevertheless, the positive valuation of external activity is lacking in its relation to the world. In addition to this, Lutheranism combines the *unio mystica* with that deep feeling of sin-stained unworthiness which is essential to preserve the *poenitentia quotidiana* of the faithful Lutheran, thereby maintaining the humility and simplicity indispensable for the forgiveness of sins. The typical religion of the Reformed Church, on the other hand, has from the beginning repudiated both this purely inward emotional piety of Lutheranism and the Quietist escape from everything of Pascal. A real penetration of the human soul by the divine was made impossible by the absolute transcendentiality of God compared to the flesh: *finitum non est capax infiniti*. The community of the elect with their God could only take place and be perceptible to them in that God worked (*operatur*) through them and that they were conscious of it. That is, their action originated from the faith caused by God's grace, and this faith in turn justified itself by the quality of

---

[48] Of course it cannot be denied that the full development of this conception did not take place until late Lutheran times (*Prætorius*, Nicolai, Meisner).

that action. Deep lying differences of the most important conditions of salvation" which apply to the classification of all practical religious activity appear here. The religious believer can make himself sure of his state of grace either in that he feels himself to be the vessel of the Holy Spirit or the tool of the divine will. In the former case his religious life tends to mysticism and emotionalism, in the latter to ascetic action; Luther stood close to the former type, Calvinism belonged definitely to the latter. The Calvinist also wanted to be saved *sola fide*. But since Calvin viewed all pure feelings and emotions, no matter how exalted they might seem to be, with suspicion, faith had to be proved by its objective results in order to provide a firm foundation for the *certitudo salutis*. It must be a *fides efficax*, the call to salvation an effectual calling (expression used in Savoy Declaration).

If we now ask further, by what fruits the Calvinist thought himself able to identify true faith? the answer is: by a type of Christian conduct which served to increase the glory of God. Just what does so serve is to be seen in his own will as revealed either directly through the Bible or indirectly through the purposeful order of the world which he has created (*lex naturae*).[49] Especially by comparing the condition of one's own soul with that of the elect, for instance the patriarchs, according to the Bible, could the state of one's own grace be known.[50] Only one of the elect really has the *fides efficax*,[51] only he is able by virtue of his rebirth (*regeneratio*) and the resulting sanctification (*sanctificatio*) of his whole life, to augment the glory of God by real, and not merely apparent, good works. It was through the consciousness that his conduct, at least in its fundamental character and constant ideal (*propositum obcedientiae,*), rested on a power" within himself working for the glory of God; that it is not only willed of God but rather done by God[52] that he attained

---

[49] Of the significance of this for the material content of social ethics some hint has been given. Here we are interested not in the content, but in the motives of moral action.

[50] How this idea must have promoted the penetration of Puritanism with the Old Testament Hebrew spirit is evident.

[51] Thus the Savoy Declaration says of the members of the *ecclesia pura* that they are "saints by effectual calling, visibly manifested by their profession and walking."

[52] Conversion is, as Sedgwick puts it, an "exact copy of the decree of predestination." And whoever is chosen is also called to obedience and made

the highest good towards which this religion strove, the certainty of salvation. That it was attainable was proved by 2 Cor. xiii- 5.19. Thus, however useless good works might be as a means of attaining salvation, for even the elect remain beings of the flesh, and everything they do falls infinitely short of divine standards, nevertheless, they are indispensable as a sign of election." They are the technical means, not of purchasing salvation, but of getting rid of the fear of damnation. In this sense they are occasionally referred to as directly necessary for salvation or the *possessio salutis* is made conditional on them.

In practice this means that God helps those who help themselves. Thus the Calvinist, as it is sometimes put, himself creates[53] his own salvation, or, as would be more correct, the conviction of it. But this creation cannot, as in Catholicism, consist in a gradual accumulation of individual good works to one's credit, but rather in a systematic self-control which at every moment stands before the inexorable alternative, chosen or damned. This brings us to a very important point in our investigation.

It is common knowledge that Lutherans have again and again accused this line of thought, which was worked out in the Reformed Churches and sects with increasing clarity,[54] of reversion to the doctrine of salvation by works. And however justified the protest of the accused against identification of their dogmatic position with the Catholic doctrine, this accusation has surely been made with reason if by it is meant the practical consequences for the everyday life of the average Christian of the Reformed Church." For a more intensive form of the religious valuation of moral action than that to which

---

capable of it, teaches Bailey. Only those whom God calls to His faith (which is expressed in their conduct) are true believers, not merely temporary believers, according to the (Baptist) Confession of Hanserd Knolly.

[53] One is reminded of a saying of Goethe with essentially the same meaning: "How can a man know himself? Never by observation, but through action. Try to do your duty and you will know what is in you. And what is your duty? Your daily task."

[54] For though Calvin himself held that saintliness must appear on the surface, the dividing-line between saints and sinners must ever remain hidden from human knowledge. We must believe that where God's pure word is alive in a Church, organized and administered according to his law, some of the elect, even though we do not know them, are present.

Calvinism led its adherents has perhaps never existed. But what is important for the practical significance of this sort of salvation by works must be sought in a knowledge of the particular qualities which characterized their type of ethical conduct and distinguished it from the everyday life of an average Christian of the Middle Ages. The difference may well be formulated as follows: the normal medieval Catholic layman lived ethically, so to speak, from hand to mouth. In the first place he conscientiously fulfilled his traditional duties. But beyond that minimum his good works did not necessarily form a connected, or at least not a rationalized, system of life, but rather remained a succession of individual acts. He could use them as occasion demanded, to atone for particular sins, to better his chances for salvation, or, toward the end of his life, as a sort of insurance premium. Of course the Catholic ethic was an ethic of intentions. But the concrete *intentio* of the single act determined its value. And the single good or bad action was credited to the doer determining his temporal and eternal fate. Quite realistically the Church recognized that man was not an absolutely clearly defined unity to be judged one way or the other, but that his moral life was normally subject to conflicting motives and his action contradictory. Of course, it required as an ideal a change of life in principle. But it weakened just this requirement (for the average) by one of its most important means of power and education, the sacrament of absolution, the function of which was connected with the deepest roots of the peculiarly Catholic religion.

The rationalization of the world, the elimination of magic as a means to salvation, the Catholics had not carried nearly so far as the Puritans (and before them the Jews) had done. To the Catholic[55] the absolution of his Church was a compensation for his own imperfection. The priest was a magician who performed the miracle of transubstantiation, and who held the key to eternal life in his hand. One could turn to him in grief and penitence. He dispensed atonement, hope of grace, certainty of forgiveness, and thereby granted release from that tremendous tension to which the Calvinist was doomed by an inexorable fate, admitting of no mitigation. For him such friendly and human comforts did not exist. He could not

---

[55] And to a certain extent also to the Lutheran. Luther did not wish to eliminate this last vestige of sacramental magic.

hope to atone for hours of weakness or of thoughtlessness by increased good will at other times, as the Catholic or even the Lutheran could. The God of Calvinism demanded of his believers not single good works, but a life of good works combined into a unified system." There was no place for the very human Catholic cycle of sin, repentance, atonement, release, followed by renewed sin. Nor was there any balance of merit for a life as a whole which could be adjusted by temporal punishments or the Churches' means of grace.

The moral conduct of the average man was thus deprived of its planless and unsystematic character and subjected to a consistent method for conduct as a whole. It is no accident that the name of Methodists stuck to the participants in the last great revival of Puritan ideas in the eighteenth century just as the term Precisians, which has the same meaning, was applied to their spiritual ancestors in the seventeenth century. For only by a fundamental change in the whole meaning of life at every moment and in every action could the effects of grace transforming a man from the *status naturae*, to the *status gratiae* be proved.

The life of the saint was directed solely toward a transcendental end, salvation. But precisely for that reason it was thoroughly rationalized in this world and dominated entirely by the aim to add to the glory of God on earth. Never has the precept *omnia in majorem dei gloriam* been taken with more bitter seriousness.[56] Only a life guided by constant thought could achieve conquest over the state of nature. Descartes's *cogito ergo sum* was taken over by the contemporary Puritans with this ethical reinterpretation. It was this rationalization which gave the Reformed faith its peculiar ascetic tendency, and is the basis both of its relationship to and its conflict with Catholicism. For naturally similar things were not unknown to Catholicism.

Without doubt Christian asceticism, both outwardly and in its inner meaning, contains many different things. But it has had a definitely rational character in its highest Occidental forms as early as the Middle Ages, and in several forms even in antiquity. The great historical significance of Western monasticism, as contrasted

---

[56] Therein lies the distinction from the mere Legality and Civility which Bunyan has living as associates of Mr. Worldly-Wiseman in the City called Morality.

with that of the Orient, is based on this fact, not in all cases, but in its general type. In the rules of St. Benedict, still more with the monks of Cluny, again with the Cistercians, and most strongly the Jesuits, it has become emancipated from plan-less, otherworldliness and irrational self-torture. It had developed a systematic method of rational conduct with the purpose of overcoming the *status naturae*, to free man from the power of irrational impulses and his dependence on the world and on nature. It attempted to subject man to the supremacy of a purposeful will, to bring his actions under constant self-control with a careful consideration of their ethical consequences. Thus it trained the monk, objectively, as a worker in the service of the kingdom of God, and thereby further, subjectively, assured the salvation of his soul. This active self-control, which formed the end of the *exercitia* of St. Ignatius and of the rational monastic virtues everywhere was also the most important practical ideal of Puritanism. In the deep contempt with which the cool reserve of its adherents is contrasted, in the reports of the trials of its martyrs, with the undisciplined blustering of the noble prelates and officials[57] can be seen that respect for quiet self-control which still distinguishes the best type of English or American gentleman today. To put it in our terms: The Puritan, like every rational type of asceticism, tried to enable a man to maintain and act upon his constant motives, especially those which it g in itself, against the emotions. In this formal psychological sense of the term it tried to make him into a personality. Contrary to many popular ideas, the end of this asceticism was to be able to lead an alert, intelligent life: the most urgent task the destruction of spontaneous, impulsive enjoyment, the most important means was to bring order into the conduct of its adherents. All these important points are emphasized in the rules of Catholic monasticism as strongly[58] as in the principles of conduct of the Calvinists."E On this methodical control over the whole man rests the enormous expansive power of both, especially

---

[57] So in the many reports of the trials of Puritan heretics cited in Neal's *History of the Puritans* and Crosby's *English Baptists*.

[58] Only not so unmixed. Contemplation, sometimes combined with emotionalism, is often combined with these rational elements. But again contemplation itself is methodically regulated.

the ability of Calvinism as against Lutheranism to defend the cause of Protestantism as the Church militant.

On the other hand, the difference of the Calvinistic from the medieval asceticism is evident. It consisted in the disappearance of the *consilia evangelica* and the accompanying transformation of asceticism to activity within the world. It is not as though Catholicism had restricted the methodical life to monastic cells. This was by no means the case either in theory or in practice. On the contrary, it has already been pointed out that, in spite of the greater ethical moderation of Catholicism, an ethically unsystematic life did not satisfy the highest ideals which it had set up even for the life of the layman.[F] The tertiary order of St. Francis was, for instance, a powerful attempt in the direction of an ascetic penetration of everyday life, and, as we know, by no means the only one. But, in fact, works like the Nachfolge Christi show, through the manner in which their strong influence was exerted, that the way of life preached in them was felt to be something higher than the everyday morality which sufficed as a minimum, and that this latter was not measured by such standards as Puritanism demanded. Moreover, the practical use made of certain institutions of the Church, above all of indulgences inevitably counteracted the tendencies toward systematic worldly asceticism. For that reason it was not felt at the time of the Reformation to be merely an unessential abuse, but one of the most fundamental evils of the Church.

But the most important thing was the fact that the man who, par excellence, lived a rational life in the religious sense was, and remained, alone the monk. Thus asceticism, the more strongly it gripped an individual, simply served to drive him farther away from everyday life, because the holiest task was definitely to surpass all worldly morality. Luther, who was not in any sense fulfilling any law of development, but acting upon his quite personal experience, which was, though at first somewhat uncertain in its practical consequences, later pushed farther by the political situation, had repudiated that tendency, and Calvinism simply took this over from him. Sebastian Franck struck the central characteristic of this type of religion when he saw the significance of the Reformation in the fact that now every Christian had to be a monk all his life. The drain of asceticism from everyday worldly life had been stopped by a dam, and those passionately spiritual natures which had formerly supplied the highest type of monk were now forced to pursue their ascetic ideals within mundane occupations.

But in the course of its development Calvinism added something positive to this, the idea of the necessity of proving one's faith in worldly activity. Therein it gave the broader groups of religiously inclined people a positive incentive to asceticism. By founding its ethic in the doctrine of predestination, it substituted for the spiritual aristocracy of monks outside of and above the world the spiritual aristocracy of the predestined saints of God within the world. It was an aristocracy which, with its character *indelebilis*, was divided from the eternally damned remainder of humanity by a more impassable and in its invisibility more terrifying gulf, than separated the monk of the Middle Ages from the rest of the world about him, a gulf which penetrated all social relations with its sharp brutality. This consciousness of divine grace of the elect and holy was accompanied by an attitude toward the sin of one's neighbor, not of sympathetic understanding based on consciousness of one's own weakness, but of hatred and contempt for him as an enemy of God bearing the signs of eternal damnation. This sort of feeling was capable of such intensity that it sometimes resulted in the formation of sects. This was the case when, as in the Independent movement of the seventeenth century, the genuine Calvinist doctrine that the glory of God required the Church to bring the damned under the law, was outweighed by the conviction that it was an insult to God if an unregenerate soul should be admitted to His house and partake in the sacraments, or even, as a minister, administer them. Thus, as a consequence of the doctrine of proof, the Donatist idea of the Church appeared, as in the case of the Calvinistic Baptists. The full logical consequence of the demand for a pure Church, a community of those proved to be in a state of grace, was not often drawn by forming sects. Modifications in the constitution of the Church resulted from the attempt to separate regenerate from unregenerate Christians, those who were from those who were not prepared for the sacrament, to keep the government of the Church or some other privilege in the hands of the former, and only to ordain ministers of whom there was no question.

The norm by which it could always measure itself, of which it was evidently in need, this asceticism naturally found in the Bible. It is important to note that the well-known bibliocracy of the Calvinists held the moral precepts of the Old Testament, since it was fully as authentically revealed, on the same level of esteem as those of the New. It was only necessary that they should not obviously be applicable only to the historical circumstances of the Hebrews, or have been specifically denied by Christ. For the believer, the law was an ideal though never quite attainable normal while Luther, on the other hand, originally had prized freedom from subjugation to the law as a divine privilege of the believer. The influence of the God-fearing but perfectly unemotional wisdom of the Hebrews, which is expressed in the books most read by the Puritans, the Proverbs and the Psalms, can be felt in their whole attitude toward life. In particular, its rational suppression of the mystical, in fact the whole emotional side of religion, has rightly been attributed by Sanford to the influence of the Old Testament. But this Old Testament rationalism was as such essentially of a small bourgeois, traditionalistic type, and was mixed not only with the powerful pathos of the prophets, but also with elements which encouraged the development of a peculiarly emotional type of religion even in the Middle Ages.[59] It was thus in the last analysis the peculiar, fundamentally ascetic, character of Calvinism itself which made it select and assimilate those elements of Old Testament religion which suited it best.

Now that systematization of ethical conduct which the asceticism of Calvinistic Protestantism had in common with the rational forms of life in the Catholic orders is expressed quite superficially in the way in which the conscientious Puritan continually supervised his own state of grace. To be sure, the religious account-books in which sins, temptations, and progress made in grace were entered or tabulated were common to both the most enthusiastic Reformed circle and some parts of modern Catholicism (especially in France), above all under the influence of the Jesuits. But in Catholicism it served the purpose of completeness of the confession, or gave the

---

[59] Among them the Song of Songs is especially noteworthy. It was for the most part simply ignored by the Puritans. Its Oriental eroticism has influenced the development of certain types of religion, such as that of St. Bernard.

directeur de l'ame[60] a basis for his authoritarian guidance of the Christian (mostly female). The Reformed Christian, however, felt his own pulse with its aid. It is mentioned by all the moralists and theologians, while Benjamin Franklin's tabulated statistical bookkeeping on his progress in the different virtues is a classic example.

On the other hand, the old medieval (even ancient) idea of God's bookkeeping is carried by Bunyan to the characteristically tasteless extreme of comparing the relation of a sinner to his God with that of customer and shopkeeper. One who has once got into debt may well, by the product of all his virtuous acts, succeed in paying off the accumulated interest but never the principal. As he observed his own conduct, the later Puritan also observed that of God and saw His finger in all the details of life. And, contrary to the strict doctrine of Calvin, he always knew why God took this or that measure. The process of sanctifying life could thus almost take on the character of a business enterprise. A thoroughgoing Christianization of the whole of life was the consequence of this methodical quality of ethical conduct into which Calvinism as distinct from Lutheranism forced men. That this rationality was decisive in its influence on practical life must always be borne in mind in order rightly to understand the influence of Calvinism. On the one hand we can see that it took this element to exercise such an influence at all. But other faiths as well necessarily bad a similar influence when their ethical motives were the same in this decisive point, the doctrine of proof.

So far we have considered only Calvinism, and have thus assumed the doctrine of predestination as the dogmatic background of the Puritan morality in the sense of methodically rationalized ethical conduct. This could be done because the influence of that dogma in fact extended far beyond the single religious group which held in all respects strictly to Calvinistic principles, the Presbyterians. Not only the Independent Savoy Declaration of 1658, but also the Baptist Confession of Hanserd Knolly of 1689 contained it, and it had a place within Methodism. Although John Wesley, the great organizing genius of the movement, was a believer in the universality of Grace, one of the great agitators of the first generation of Methodists and their most consistent thinker,

---

[60] Manager of the soul -

Whitefield, was an adherent of the doctrine. The same was true of the circle around Lady Huntingdon, which for a time had considerable influence. It was this doctrine in its magnificent consistency which, in the fateful epoch of the seventeenth century, upheld the belief of the militant defenders of the holy life that they were weapons in the hand of God, and executors of His providential will.[61] Moreover, it prevented a premature collapse into a purely utilitarian doctrine of good works in this world which would never have been capable of motivating such tremendous sacrifices for non-rational ideal ends.

The combination of faith in absolutely valid norms with absolute determinism and the complete transcendentality of God was in its way a product of great genius. At the same time it was, in principle, very much more modern than the milder doctrine. Making greater concessions to the feelings which subjected God to the moral law. Above all, we shall see again and again how fundamental is the idea of proof for our problem. Since its practical significance as a psychological basis for rational morality could be studied in such purity in the doctrine of predestination, it was best to start there with the doctrine in its most consistent form. But it forms a recurring framework. for the connection between faith and conduct in the denominations to be studied below. Within the Protestant movement the consequences which it inevitably had for the ascetic tendencies of the conduct of its first adherents form in principle the strongest antithesis to the relative moral helplessness of Lutheranism. The Lutheran *gratia amissibilis*, which could always be regained through penitent contrition evidently, in itself, contained no sanction for what is for us the most important result of ascetic Protestantism, a systematic rational ordering of the moral life as a whole. The Lutheran faith thus left the spontaneous vitality of impulsive action and naïve emotion more nearly unchanged. The motive to constant self-control and thus to a deliberate regulation of one's own life, which the gloomy doctrine of Calvinism gave, was lacking. A religious genius like Luther could live in this atmosphere of openness and freedom without difficulty and, so long as his enthusiasm was powerful enough, without danger of falling back

---

[61] In contrast to that, Luther himself said: "Weeping goes before action and suffering excels all accomplishment"

into the *status naturalis*. That simple, sensitive, and peculiarly emotional form of piety, which is the ornament of many of the highest types of Lutherans, like their free and spontaneous morality, finds few parallels in genuine Puritanism, but many more in the mild Anglicanism of such men as Hooker, Chillingsworth, etc. But for the everyday Lutheran, even the able one, nothing was more certain than that he was only temporarily, as long as the single confession or sermon affected him, raised above the *status naturalis*. There was a great difference which was very striking to contemporaries between the moral standards of the courts of Reformed and of Lutheran princes, the latter often being degraded by drunkenness and vulgarity.

Moreover, the helplessness of the Lutheran clergy, with their emphasis on faith alone, against the ascetic Baptist movement, is well known. The typical German quality often called good nature (Gemutlichkeit) or naturalness contrasts strongly, even in the facial expressions of people, with the effects of that thorough destruction of the spontaneity of the *status naturalis* in the Anglo-American atmosphere, which Germans are accustomed to judge unfavorably as narrowness, unfreeness, and inner constraint. But the differences of conduct, which are very striking, have clearly originated in the lesser degree of ascetic penetration of life in Lutheranism as distinguished from Calvinism. The antipathy of every spontaneous child of nature to everything ascetic is expressed in those feelings. The fact is that Lutheranism, on account of its doctrine of grace, lacked a psychological sanction of systematic conduct to compel the methodical rationalization of life.

This sanction, which conditions the ascetic character of religion, could doubtless in itself have been furnished by various different religious motives, as we shall soon see. The Calvinistic doctrine of predestination was only one of several possibilities. But nevertheless we have become convinced that in its way it had not only a quite unique consistency, but that its psychological effect was extraordinarily powerful. In comparison with it the non-Calvinistic ascetic movements, considered purely from the viewpoint of the religious motivation of asceticism, form an attenuation of the inner consistency and power of Calvinism.

But even in the actual historical development the situation was, for the most part, such that the Calvinistic form of asceticism was either imitated by the other ascetic movements or used as a source of inspiration or of comparison in the development of their divergent principles. Where, in spite of a different doctrinal basis, similar ascetic features have appeared, this has generally been the result of Church organization. Of this we shall come to speak in another connection.

B. PIETISM

Historically the doctrine of predestination is also the starting-point of the ascetic movement usually known as Pietism. In so far as the movement remained within the Reformed Church, it is almost impossible to draw the line between Pietistic and non-Pietistic Calvinists. Almost all the leading representatives of Puritanism are sometimes classed among the Pietists. It is even quite legitimate to look upon the whole connection between predestination and the doctrine of proof, with its fundamental interest in the attainment of the *certitudo salutis* as discussed above, as in itself a Pietistic development of Calvin's original doctrines. The occurrence of ascetic revivals within the Reformed Church was, especially in Holland, regularly accompanied by a regeneration of the doctrine of predestination which had been temporarily forgotten or not strictly held to. Hence for England it is not customary to use the term Pietism at all.

But even the Continental (Dutch and Lower Rhenish) Pietism in the Reformed Church was, at least fundamentally, just as much a simple intensification of the Reformed asceticism as, for instance, the doctrines of Bailey. The emphasis was placed so strongly on the *praxis pietatis* that doctrinal orthodoxy was pushed into the background; at times, in fact, it seemed quite a matter of indifference. Those predestined for grace could occasionally be subject to dogmatic error as well as to other sins and experience showed that often those Christians who were quite uninstructed in the theology of the schools exhibited the fruits of faith most clearly, while on the other hand it became evident that mere knowledge of theology by no means guaranteed the proof of faith through conduct.G

Thus election could not be proved by theological learning at all. Hence Pietism, with a deep distrust of the Church of the theologians, to which this is characteristic of it – it still belonged officially, began to gather the adherents of the *praxis pietatis in conventicles* removed from the world. It wished to make the invisible Church of the elect visible on this earth. Without going so far as to form a separate sect, its members attempted to live, in this community, a life freed from all the temptations of the world and in all its details dictated by God's will, and thus to be made certain of their own rebirth by external signs manifested in their daily conduct. Thus the *ecclesiola* of the true converts — this was common to all genuinely Pietistic groups — wished, by means of intensified asceticism, to enjoy the blissfulness of community with God in this life.

Now this latter tendency had something closely, related to the Lutheran *unio mystica*, and very often led to a greater emphasis on the emotional side of religion than was acceptable to orthodox Calvinism. In fact this may, from our view-point, be said to be the decisive characteristic of the Pietism which developed within the Reformed Church. For this element of emotion, which was originally quite foreign to Calvinism, but on the other hand related to certain mediaeval forms of religion, led religion in practice to strive for the enjoyment of salvation in this world rather than to engage in the ascetic struggle for certainty about the future world. Moreover, the emotion was capable of such intensity, that religion took on a positively hysterical character, resulting in the alternation which is familiar from examples without number and neuro-pathologically understandable, of half-conscious states of religious ecstasy with periods of nervous exhaustion, which were felt as abandonment by God. The effect was the direct opposite of the strict and temperate discipline under which men were placed by the systematic life of holiness of the Puritan. It meant a weakening of the inhibitions which protected the rational personality of the Calvinist from his passions. Similarly it was possible for the Calvinistic idea of the depravity of the flesh, taken emotionally, for instance in the form of the so-called worm-feeling, to lead to a deadening of enterprise in worldly activity. Even the doctrine of predestination could lead to fatalism if, contrary to the predominant tendencies of rational Calvinism, it were made the object of emotional contemplation. Finally, the desire to separate the elect from the world could, with a strong emotional intensity, lead to a sort of monastic community life of half-communistic character, as the history of Pietism, even within the Reformed Church, has shown again and again.

But so long as this extreme effect, conditioned by this emphasis on emotion, did not appear, as long as Reformed Pietism strove to make sure of salvation within the everyday routine of life in a worldly calling, the practical effect of Pietistic principles was an even stricter ascetic control of conduct in the calling, which provided a still more solid religious basis for the ethic of the calling, than the mere worldly respectability of the normal Reformed Christian, which was felt by the superior Pietist to be a second-rate Christianity. The religious aristocracy of the elect, which developed in every form of Calvinistic asceticism, the more seriously it was taken, the more surely, was then organized, in Holland, on a voluntary basis in the form of conventicles within the Church. In English Puritanism, on the other hand, it led partly to a virtual differentiation between active and passive Christians within the Church organization, and partly, as has been shown above, to the formation of sects.

On the other hand, the development of German Pietism from a Lutheran basis, with which the names of Spener, Francke, and Zinzendorf are connected, led away from the doctrine of predestination. But at the same time it was by no means outside the body of ideas of which that dogma formed the logical climax, as is especially attested by Spener's own account of the influence which English and Dutch Pietism had upon him, and is shown by the fact that Bailey was read in his first conventicles.

From our special point of view, at any rate, Pietism meant simply the penetration of methodically controlled and supervised, thus of ascetic, conduct into the non-Calvinistic denominations." But Lutheranism necessarily felt this rational asceticism to be a foreign element, and the lack of consistency in German Pietistic doctrines was the result of the difficulties growing out of that fact. As a dogmatic basis of systematic religious conduct Spener combines Lutheran ideas with the specifically Calvinistic doctrine of good works as such which are undertaken with the "intention of doing honor to God." He also has a faith, suggestive of Calvinism, in the possibility of the elect attaining a relative degree of Christian perfection. But the theory lacked consistency. Spener, who was strongly influenced by the mystics, attempted in a rather uncertain but essentially Lutheran manner, rather to describe the systematic type of Christian conduct which was essential to even his form of Pietism than to justify it. He did not derive the *certitudo salutis* from sanctification; instead of the idea of proof, he adopted Luther's somewhat loose connection between faith and works, which has been discussed above.

But again and again, in so far as the rational and ascetic element of Pietism outweighed the emotional, the ideas essential to our thesis maintained their place. These were: (1) that the methodical development of one's own state of grace to a higher and higher degree of certainty and perfection in terms of the law was a sign of grace; and (2) that "God's Providence works through those in such a state of perfection", *i.e.* in that He gives them His signs if they wait patiently and deliberate methodically.ᴴ Labor in a calling was also the ascetic activity par excellence for A. H. Francke, that God Himself blessed His chosen ones through the success of their labors was as undeniable to him as we shall find it to have been to the Puritans.

And as a substitute for the double decree Pietism worked out ideas which, in a way essentially similar to Calvinism, though milder, established an aristocracy of the elect resting on God's especial grace, with all the psychological results pointed out above. Among them belongs, for instance, the so-called doctrine of Terminism, which was generally (though unjustly) attributed to Pietism by its opponents. It assumes that grace is offered to all men, but for everyone either once at a definite moment in his life or at some moment for the last time. Anyone who let that moment pass was beyond the help of the universality of grace; he was in the same situation as those neglected by God in the Calvinistic doctrine. Quite close to this theory was the idea which Francke took from his personal experience, and which was very widespread in Pietism, one may even say predominant, that grace could only become effective under certain unique and peculiar circumstances, namely, after previous repentance. Since, according to Pietist doctrine, not everyone was capable of such experiences, those who, in spite of the use of the ascetic methods recommended by the Pietists to bring it about, did not attain it, remained in the eyes of the regenerate a sort of passive Christian. On the other hand, by the creation, of a method to induce repentance even the attainment of divine grace became in effect an object of rational human activity.

Moreover, the antagonism to the private confessional, which, though not shared by all — for instance, not by Francke — was characteristic of many Pietists, especially as the repeated questions in Spener show, of Pieti pastors, resulted from this aristocracy of grace. This antagonism helped to weaken its ties with Lutheranism. The visible effects on conduct of grace gained through repentance formed a necessary criterion for admission to absolution; hence it was impossible to let *contritio* alone suffice. Zinzendorf's conception of his own religious position, even though it vacillated in the face of attack from orthodoxy, tended generally toward the instrumental idea. Beyond that, however, the doctrine standpoint of this remarkable religious dilettante, Ritschl calls him, is scarcely capable of clear formulation in the points of importance for us. He repeatedly designated himself a representative of Pauline-Lutheran Christianity; hence he opposed the Pietistic type associated with Jansen with its adherence to the law. But the Brotherhood itself in practice upheld, as early as its Protocol of August 22, 1729, a standpoint which in many respects closely resembled that of the Calvinistic aristocracy of the elect. And in spite of his repeated avowals of Lutheranism, he permitted and encouraged it. The famous stand of attributing the Old Testament to Christ, taken on November 2, 1741, was the outward expression of somewhat the same attitude. However, of the three branches of the Brotherhood, both the Calvinistic and the Moravian accepted the Reformed ethics in essentials from the beginning. And even Zinzendorf followed the Puritans in expressing to John Wesley the opinion that even though a man himself could not, others could know his state of grace by his conduct.

But on the other hand, in the peculiar piety of Herrnhut, the emotional element held a very prominent place. In particular Zinzendorf himself continually attempted to counteract the tendency to ascetic sanctification in the Puritan sense and to turn the interpretation of good works in a Lutheran direction. Also under the influence of the repudiation of conventicles and the retention of the confession, there developed an essentially Lutheran dependence on the sacraments. Moreover, Zinzendorf's peculiar principle that the childlikeness of religious feeling was a sign of its genuineness, as well as the use of the lot as a means of revealing God's will, strongly counteracted the influence of rationality in conduct. On the whole, within the sphere of influence of the Count,[1] the anti-rational, emotional elements predominated much more in the religion of the Herrnhuters than elsewhere in pietism. The connection between morality and the forgiveness of sins in Spangenberg's *Idea fides fratrum* is as loose as in Lutheranism generally. Zinzendorf's repudiation of the Methodist pursuit of perfection is part, here as everywhere, of his fundamentally eudemonistic ideal of having men experience eternal bliss (he calls it happiness) emotionally in the present, instead of encouraging them by rational labor to make sure of it in the next world.

Nevertheless, the idea that the most important value of the Brotherhood as contrasted with other Churches lay in an active Christian life, in missionary, and, which was brought into connection with it, in professional work in a calling, remained a vital force with them. In addition, the practical rationalization of life from the standpoint of utility was very essential to Zinzendorf's philosophy. It was derived for him, as for other Pietists, on the one hand from his decided dislike of philosophical speculation as dangerous to faith, and his corresponding preference for empirical knowledge ; on the other hand, from the shrewd common sense of the professional missionary. The Brotherhood was, as a great mission centre, at the same time a business enterprise. Thus it led its members into the paths of worldly asceticism, which everywhere first seeks for tasks and then carries them out carefully and systematically. However, the glorification of the apostolic poverty, of the disciples[J] chosen by God through predestination, which was derived from the example of the apostles as missionaries, formed another obstacle. It meant in effect a partial revival of the *consilia evangelica*. The development of a rational economic ethic similar to the Calvinistic was certainly retarded by these factors, even though, as the development of the Baptist movement shows, it was not impossible, but on the contrary subjectively strongly encouraged by the idea of work solely for the sake of the calling.

All in all, when we consider German Pietism from the point of view important for us, we must admit a vacillation and uncertainty in the religious basis of its asceticism which makes it definitely weaker than the iron consistency of Calvinism, and which is partly the result of Lutheran influences and partly of its emotional character. To be sure, it is very one-sided to make this emotional element the distinguishing characteristic of Pietism as opposed to Lutheranism. But compared to Calvinism, the rationalization of life was necessarily less intense because the pressure of occupation with a state of grace which had continually to be proved, and which was concerned for the future in eternity, was diverted to the present emotional state. The place of the self-confidence which the elect sought to attain, and continually to renew in restless and successful work at his calling, was taken by an attitude of humility and abnegation. This in turn was partly the result of emotional stimulus directed solely toward spiritual experience; partly of the Lutheran institution of the confession, which, though it was often looked upon with serious doubts by Pietism, was still generally tolerated. All this shows the influence of the peculiarly Lutheran conception of salvation by the forgiveness of sins and not by practical sanctification. In place of the systematic rational struggle to attain and retain certain knowledge of future (otherworldly) salvation comes here the need to feel reconciliation and community with God now. Thus the tendency of the pursuit of present enjoyment to hinder the rational organization of economic life, depending as it does on provision for the future, has in a certain sense a parallel in the field of religious life.

Evidently, then, the orientation of religious needs to present emotional satisfaction could not develop so powerful a motive to rationalize worldly activity, as the need of the Calvinistic elect for proof with their exclusive preoccupation with the beyond. On the other hand, it was considerably more favorable to the methodical penetration of conduct with religion than the traditionalistic faith of the orthodox Lutheran, bound as it was to the Word and the sacraments. On the whole Pietism from Francke and Spener to

Zinzendorf tended toward increasing emphasis on the emotional side. But this was not in any sense the expression of an imminent law of development. The differences resulted from differences of the religious (and social) environments from which the leaders came. We cannot enter into that here, nor can we discuss how the peculiarities of German Pietism have affected its social and geographical extension. We must again remind ourselves that this emotional Pietism of course shades off into the way of life of the Puritan elect by quite gradual stages. If we can, at least provisionally, point out any practical consequence of the difference, we may say that the virtues favored by Pietism were more those on the one hand of the faithful official, clerk, laborer, or domestic worker, and on the other of the predominantly patriarchal employer with a pious condescension (in Zinzendorf's manner). Calvinism, in comparison, appears to be more closely related to the hard legalism and the active enterprise of bourgeois-capitalistic entrepreneurs. Finally, the purely emotional form of Pietism is, as Ritschl[62] has pointed out, a religious dilettantism for the leisure classes. However far this characterization falls short of being exhaustive, it helps to explain certain differences in the character (including the economic character) of peoples which have been under the influence of one or the other of these two ascetic movements.

C. METHODISM

The combination of an emotional but still ascetic type of religion with increasing indifference to or repudiation of the dogmatic basis of Calvinistic asceticism is characteristic also of the Anglo-American movement corresponding to Continental Pietism, namely Methodism. The name in itself shows what impressed contemporaries as characteristic of its adherents: the methodical, systematic nature of conduct for the purpose of attaining the *certitudo salutis*. This was from the beginning the centre of religious aspiration for this movement also, and remained so. In spite of all

---

[62] That Frederick William I called Pietism a religion for the leisure class is more indicative of his own Pietism than that of Spener and Francke. Even this king knew very well why he had opened his realm to the Pietists by his declaration of toleration.

the differences, the undoubted relationship to certain branches of German Pietism is shown above all by the fact that the method was used primarily to bring about the emotional act of conversion. And the emphasis on feeling, in John Wesley awakened by Moravian and Lutheran influences, led Methodism, which from the beginning saw its mission among the masses, to take on a strongly emotional character, especially in America. The attainment of repentance under certain circumstances involved an emotional struggle of such intensity as to lead to the most terrible ecstasies, which in America often took place in a public meeting. This formed the basis of a belief in the undeserved possession of divine grace and at the same time of an immediate consciousness of justification and forgiveness.

Now this emotional religion entered into a peculiar alliance, containing no small inherent difficulties, with the ascetic ethics which had for good and all been stamped with rationality by Puritanism. For one thing, unlike Calvinism, which held everything emotional to be illusory, the only sure basis for the *certitudo salutis* was in principle held to be a pure feeling of absolute certainty of forgiveness, derived immediately from the testimony of the spirit, the coming of which could be definitely placed to the hour. Added to this is Wesley's doctrine of sanctification which, though a decided departure from the orthodox doctrine, is a logical development of it. According to it, one reborn in this manner can, by virtue of the divine grace already working in him, even in this life attain sanctification, the consciousness of perfection in the sense of freedom from sin, by a second, generally separate and often sudden spiritual transformation. However difficult of attainment this end is, generally not till toward the end of one's life, it must inevitably be sought, because it finally guarantees the *certitudo salutis* and substitutes a serene confidence for the sullen worry of the Calvinist. And it distinguishes the true convert in his own eyes and those of others by the fact that sin at least no longer has power over him.

In spite of the great significance of self-evident feeling, righteous conduct according to the law was thus naturally also adhered to. Whenever Wesley attacked the emphasis on works of his time, it was only to revive the old Puritan doctrine that works are not the cause, but only the means of knowing one's state of grace, and even this only when they are performed solely for the glory of God.

Righteous conduct alone did not suffice, as he had found out for himself. The feeling of grace was necessary in addition. He himself sometimes described works as a condition of grace, and in the Declaration of August 9, 1771, he emphasized that he who performed no good works was not a true believer. In fact, the Methodists have always maintained that they did not differ from the Established Church in doctrine, but only in religious practice. This emphasis on the fruits of belief was mostly justified by I John iii, 9; conduct is taken as a clear sign of rebirth.

But in spite of all that there were difficulties. For those Methodists who were adherents of the doctrine of predestination, to think of the *certitudo salutis* as appearing in the immediate feeling of grace and perfection instead of the consciousness of grace which grew out of ascetic conduct in continual proof of faith since then the certainty of the *perservantia* depended only on the single act of repentance meant one of two things. For weak natures there was a fatalistic interpretation of Christian freedom, and with it the breakdown of methodical conduct; or, where this path was rejected, the self-confidence of the righteous man reached untold heights, an emotional intensification of the Puritan type. In the face of the attacks of opponents, the attempt was made to meet these consequences. On the one hand by increased emphasis on the normative authority of the Bible and the indispensability of proof; on the other by, in effect, strengthening Wesley's anti-Calvinistic faction within the movement with its doctrine that grace could be lost. The strong Lutheran influences to which Wesley was exposed through the Moravians strengthened this tendency and increased the uncertainty of the religious basis of the Methodist ethics. In the end only the concept of regeneration, an emotional certainty of salvation as the immediate result of faith, was definitely maintained as the indispensable foundation of grace; and with it sanctification, resulting in (at least virtual) freedom from the power of sin, as the consequent proof of grace. The significance of external means of grace, especially the sacraments, was correspondingly diminished. In any case, the general awakening which followed Methodism everywhere, for example in New England, meant a victory for the doctrine of grace and election.

Thus from our view-point the Methodist ethic appears to rest on a foundation of uncertainty similar to Pietism. But the aspiration to the higher life, the second blessedness, served it as a sort of makeshift for the doctrine of predestination. Moreover, being English in origin, its ethical practice was closely related to that of English Puritanism, the revival of which it aspired to be. The emotional act of conversion was methodically induced. And after it was attained there did not follow a pious enjoyment of community with God, after the manner of the emotional Pietism of Zinzendorf, but the emotion, once awakened, was directed into a rational struggle for perfection. Hence the emotional character of its faith did not lead to a spiritualized religion of feeling like German Pietism. It has already been shown by Schneckenburger that this fact was connected with the less intensive development of the sense of sin (partly directly on account of the emotional experience of conversion), and this has remained an accepted point in the discussion of Methodism. The fundamentally Calvinistic character of its religious feeling here remained decisive. The emotional excitement took the form of enthusiasm which was only occasionally, but then powerfully stirred, but which by no means destroyed the otherwise rational character of conduct.[K] The regeneration of Methodism thus created only a supplement to the pure doctrine of works, a religious basis for ascetic conduct after the doctrine of predestination had been given up. The signs given by conduct which formed an indispensable means of ascertaining true conversion, even its condition as Wesley occasionally says, were in fact just the same as those of Calvinism. As a late product we can, in the following discussion, generally neglect Methodism, as it added nothing new to the development of the idea of calling.

D. THE BAPTIST SECTS

The Pietism of the Continent of Europe and the Methodism of the Anglo-Saxon peoples are, considered both in their content of ideas and their historical significance, secondary movements. On the other hand, we find a second independent source of Protestant asceticism besides Calvinism in the Baptist movement and the sects which, in the course of the sixteenth and seventeenth centuries, came directly from it or adopted its forms of religious thought, the Baptists, Mennonites, and, above all, the Quakers. With them we approach religious groups whose ethics rest upon a basis differing in principle from the Calvinistic doctrine. The following sketch, which only emphasizes what is important for us, can give no true impression of the diversity of this movement. Again we lay the principal emphasis on the development in the older capitalistic countries.

The feature of all these communities, which is both historically and in principle most important, but whose influence on the development of culture can only be made quite clear in a somewhat different connection, is something with which we are already familiar, the believer's Church. This means that the religious community, the visible Church in the language of the Reformation Churches, was no longer looked upon as a sort of trust foundation for supernatural ends, an institution, necessarily including both the just and the unjust, whether for increasing the glory of God (Calvinistic) or as a medium for bringing the means of salvation to men (Catholic and Lutheran), but solely as a community of personal believers of the reborn, and only these. In other words, not as a Church but as a Sect.[L] This is all that the principle, in itself purely external, that only adults who have personally gained their own faith should be baptized, is meant to symbolize.[63] The justification through this faith was for the Baptists, as they have insistently repeated in all religious discussions, radically different from the idea of work in the world in the service of Christ, such as dominated the orthodox dogma of the older Protestantism. It consisted rather in taking spiritual possession of His gift of salvation. But this occurred through individual revelation, by the working of the Divine Spirit in the individual, and only in that way. It was offered to everyone, and it sufficed to wait for the Spirit, and not to resist its coming by a sinful attachment to the world. The significance of faith in the sense of knowledge of the doctrines of the Church, but also in that of a repentant search for divine grace, was consequently quite minimized, and there took place, naturally with great modifications, a renaissance of Early Christian pneumatic doctrines. For instance, the sect to which Menno Simons in his *Fondamentboek* gave the first

---

[63] How important this symbol was, historically, for the conservation of the Church community, since it was an unambiguous and unmistakable sign.

reasonably consistent doctrine, wished, like the other Baptist sects, to be the true blameless Church of Christ; like the apostolic community, consisting entirely of those personally awakened and called by God. Those who have been born again, and they alone, are brethren of Christ, because they, like Him, have been created in spirit directly by God. A strict avoidance of the world, in the sense of all not strictly necessary intercourse with worldly people, together with the strictest bibliocracy in the sense of taking the life of the first generations of Christians as a model, were the results for the first Baptist communities, and this principle of avoidance of the world never quite disappeared so long as the old spirit remained alive.

As a permanent possession, the Baptist sects retained from these dominating motives of their early period a principle with which, on a somewhat different foundation, we have already become acquainted in Calvinism, and the fundamental importance of which will again and again come out. They absolutely repudiated all idolatry of the flesh, as a detraction from the reverence due to God alone.[M] The Biblical way of life was conceived by the first Swiss and South German Baptists with a radicalism similar to that of the young St. Francis, as a sharp break with all the enjoyment of life, a life modeled directly on that of the Apostles. And, in truth, the life of many of the earlier Baptists is reminiscent of that of St. Giles. But this strict observation of Biblical precepts was not on very secure foundations in its connection with the pneumatic character of the faith. What God had revealed to the prophets and apostles was not all that He could and would reveal. On the contrary, the continued life of the Word, not as a written document, but as the force of the Holy Spirit working in daily life, which speaks directly to any individual who is willing to hear, was the sole characteristic of the true Church. That, as Schwenkfeld taught as against Luther and later Fox against the Presbyterians, was the testimony of the early Christian communities. From this idea of the continuance of revelation developed the well-known doctrine, later consistently worked out by the Quakers, of the (in the last analysis decisive) significance of the inner testimony of the Spirit in reason and conscience. This did away, not with the authority, but with the sole authority, of the Bible, and started a development which in the end radically eliminated all that remained of the doctrine of salvation through the Church; for the Quakers even with Baptism and the Communion.

The Baptist denominations along with the predestinationists, especially the strict Calvinists, carried out the most radical devaluation of all sacraments as means to salvation, and thus accomplished the religious rationalization of the world in its most extreme form. Only the inner light of continual revelation could enable one truly to understand even the Biblical revelations of God. On the other hand, at least according to the Quaker doctrine which here drew the logical conclusion, its effects could be extended to people who had never known revelation in its Biblical form. The proposition *extra ecclesiam nulla salus* held only for this invisible Church of those illuminated by the Spirit. Without the inner light, the natural man, even the man guided by natural reason, remained purely a creature of the flesh, whose godlessness was condemned by the Baptists, including the Quakers, almost even more harshly than by the Calvinists. On the other hand, the new birth caused by the Spirit, if we wait for it and open our hearts to it, may, since it is divinely caused, lead to a state of such complete conquest of the power of sin that relapses, to say nothing of the loss of the state of grace, become practically impossible. However, as in Methodism at a later time, the attainment of that state was not thought of as the rule, but rather the degree of perfection of the individual was subject to development.

But all Baptist communities desired to be pure Churches in the sense of the blameless conduct of their members. A sincere repudiation of the world and its interests, and unconditional submission to God as speaking through the conscience, were the only unchallengeable signs of true rebirth, and a corresponding type of conduct was thus indispensable to salvation. And hence the gift of God's grace could not be earned, but only one who followed the dictates of his conscience could be justified in considering himself reborn. Good works in this sense were a *causa sine qua non*. As we see, this last reasoning of Barclay, to whose exposition we have adhered, was again the equivalent in practice of the Calvinistic doctrine, and was certainly developed under the influence of the Calvinistic asceticism, which surrounded the Baptist sects in England and the Netherlands. George Fox devoted the whole of his early missionary activity to the preaching of its earnest and sincere adoption.

But, since predestination was rejected, the peculiarly rational character of Baptist morality rested psychologically above all on the idea of expectant waiting for the Spirit to descend, which even today is characteristic of the Quaker meeting, and is well analyzed by Barclay. The purpose of this silent waiting is to overcome everything impulsive and irrational, the passions and subjective interests of the natural man. He must be stilled in order to create that deep repose of the soul in which alone the word of God can be heard. Of course, this waiting might result in hysterical conditions, prophecy, and, as long as eschatological hopes survived, under certain circumstances even in an outbreak of chiliastic enthusiasm, as is possible in all similar types of religion. That actually happened in the movement which went to pieces in Munster.

But in so far as Baptism affected the normal workaday world, the idea that God only speaks when the flesh is silent evidently meant an incentive to the deliberate weighing of courses of action and their careful justification in terms of the individual conscience. The later Baptist communities, most particularly the Quakers, adopted this quiet, moderate, eminently conscientious character of conduct. The radical elimination of magic from the world allowed no other psychological course than the practice of worldly asceticism. Since these communities would have nothing to do with the political powers and their doings, the external result also was the penetration of life in the calling with these ascetic virtues. The leaders of the earliest Baptist movement were ruthlessly radical in their rejection of worldliness. But naturally, even in the first generation, the strictly apostolic way of life was not maintained as absolutely essential to the proof of rebirth for everyone. Well-to-do bourgeois there were, even in this generation and even before Menno, who definitely defended the practical worldly virtues and the system of private property; the strict morality of the Baptists had turned in practice into the path prepared by the Calvinistic ethic. This was simply because the road to the otherworldly monastic form of asceticism had been closed as unbiblical and savoring of salvation by works since Luther, whom the Baptists also followed in this respect.

Nevertheless, apart from the half-communistic communities of the early period, one Baptist sect, the so-called Dunckards (*Tunker, dompelaers*), has to this day maintained its condemnation of education and of every form of possession beyond that indispensable to life. And even Barclay looks upon the obligation to one's calling not in Calvinistic or even Lutheran terms, but rather Thomistically, as *naturali ratione*, the necessary consequence of the believers, having to live in the world.

This attitude meant a weakening of the Calvinistic conception of the calling similar to those of Spener and the German Pietists. But, on the other hand, the intensity of interest in economic occupations was considerably increased by various factors at work in the Baptist sects. In the first place, by the refusal to accept office in the service of the State, which originated as a religious duty following from the repudiation of everything worldly. After its abandonment in principle it still remained, at least for the Mennonites and Quakers, effective in practice, because the strict refusal to bear arms or to take oaths formed a sufficient disqualification for office. Hand in hand with it in all Baptists' denominations went an invincible antagonism to any sort of aristocratic way of life. Partly, as with the Calvinists, it was a consequence of the prohibition of all idolatry of the flesh, partly a result of the aforementioned unpolitical or even anti-political principles. The whole shrewd and conscientious rationality of Baptist conduct was thus forced into non-political callings.

At the same time, the immense importance which was attributed by the Baptist doctrine of salvation to the role of the conscience as the revelation of God to the individual gave their conduct in worldly callings a character which was of the greatest significance for the development of the spirit of capitalism. We shall have to postpone its consideration until later, and it can then be studied only in so far as this is possible without entering into the whole political and social ethics of Protestant asceticism. But, to anticipate this much, we have already called attention to that most important principle of the capitalistic ethic which is generally formulated "honesty is the best policy."[64] Its classical document is the tract of Franklin quoted

---

[64] Veblen in his suggestive book *The Theory of Business Enterprise* is of the opinion that this motto belongs only to early capitalism. But economic supermen, who, like the present captains of industry, have stood beyond good and evil, have

above. And even in the judgment of the seventeenth century the specific form of the worldly asceticism of the Baptists, especially the Quakers, lay in the practical adoption of this maxim. On the other hand, we shall expect to find that the influence of Calvinism was exerted more in the direction of the liberation of energy for private acquisition. For in spite of all the formal legalism of the elect, Goethe's remark in fact applied often enough to the Calvinist: "The man of action is always ruthless; no one has a conscience but an observer."

A further important element which promoted the intensity of the worldly asceticism of the Baptist denominations can in its full significance also be considered only in another connection. Nevertheless, we may anticipate a few remarks on it to justify the order of presentation we have chosen. We have quite deliberately not taken as a starting point the objective social institutions of the older Protestant Churches, and their ethical influences, especially not the very important Church discipline. We have preferred rather to take the results which subjective adoption of an ascetic faith might have had in the conduct of the individual. This was not only because this side of the thing has previously received far less attention than the other, but also because the effect of Church discipline was by no means always a similar one. On the contrary, the ecclesiastical supervision of the life of the individual, which, as it was practiced in the Calvinistic State Churches, almost amounted to an inquisition, might even retard that liberation of individual powers which was conditioned by the rational ascetic pursuit of salvation, and in some cases actually did so.

The mercantilistic regulations of the State might develop industries, but not, or certainly not alone, the spirit of capitalism; where they assumed a despotic, authoritarian character, they to a large extent directly hindered it. Thus a similar effect might well have resulted from ecclesiastical regimentation when it became excessively despotic. It enforced a particular type of external conformity, but in some cases weakened the subjective motives of rational conduct. Any discussion of this point must take account of the great difference between the results of the authoritarian moral

---

always existed, and the statement is still true of the broad underlying strata of business men.

discipline of the Established Churches and tile corresponding discipline in the sects which rested on voluntary submission. That the Baptist movement everywhere and in principle founded sects and not Churches was certainly as favorable to the intensity of their asceticism as was the case, to differing degrees, with those Calvinistic, Methodist, and Pietist communities which were driven by their situations into the formation of voluntary groups.[65]

It is our next task to follow out the results of the Puritan idea of the calling in the business world, now that the above sketch has attempted to show its religious foundations. With all the differences of detail and emphasis which these different ascetic movements show in the aspects with which we have been concerned, much the same characteristics are present and important in all of them. But for our purposes the decisive point was, to recapitulate, the conception of the state of religious grace, common to all the denominations, as a status which marks off its possessor from the degradation of the flesh, from the world.

On the other hand, though the means by which it was attained differed for different doctrines, it could not be guaranteed by any magical sacraments, by relief in the confession, nor by individual good works. That was only possible by proof in a specific type of conduct unmistakably different from the way of life of the natural man. From that followed for the individual an incentive methodically to supervise his own state of grace in his own conduct, and thus to penetrate it with asceticism. But, as we have seen, this ascetic conduct meant a rational planning of the whole of one's life in accordance with God's will. And this asceticism was no longer an *opus supererogationis*, but something which could be required of everyone who would be certain of salvation. The religious life of the saints, as distinguished from the natural life, was the most important point, no longer lived outside the world in monastic communities, but within the world and its institutions. This rationalization of conduct within this world, but for the sake of the world beyond, was the consequence of the concept of calling of ascetic Protestantism.

Christian asceticism, at first fleeing from the world into solitude, had already ruled the world which it had renounced from the

---

[65] This is the reason for the economic importance of the ascetic Protestant, but not Catholic, minorities.

monastery and through the Church. But it had, on the whole, left the naturally spontaneous character of daily life in the world untouched. Now it strode into the marketplace of life, slammed the door of the monastery behind it, and undertook to penetrate just that daily routine of life with its methodicalness, to fashion it into a life in the world, but neither of nor for this world. With what result, we shall try to make clear in the following discussion.

Chapter V

Asceticism *and the* Spirit *of* Capitalism

I n order to understand the connection between the fundamental religious ideas of ascetic Protestantism and its maxims for everyday economic conduct, it is necessary to examine with especial care such writings as have evidently been derived from ministerial practice. For in a time in which the beyond meant everything, when the social position of the Christian depended upon his admission to the communion, the clergyman, through his ministry, Church discipline, and preaching, exercised an influence (as a glance at collections of *consilia, casus conscientia,* etc., shows) which we modern men are entirely unable to picture. In such a time the religious forces which express themselves through such channels are the decisive influences in the formation of national character.

For the purposes of this chapter, though by no means for all purposes, we can treat ascetic Protestantism as a single whole. But since that side of English Puritanism which was derived from Calvinism gives the most consistent religious basis for the idea of the calling, we shall, following our previous method, place one of its representatives at the centre of the discussion. Richard Baxter stands out above many other writers on Puritan ethics, both because of his eminently practical and realistic attitude, and, at the same time, because of the universal recognition accorded to his works, which have gone through many new editions and translations. He was a Presbyterian and an apologist of the Westminster Synod, but at the same time, like so many of the best spirits of his time, gradually grew away from the dogmas of pure Calvinism. At heart he opposed Cromwell's usurpation as he would any revolution. He was unfavorable to the sects and the fanatical enthusiasm of the saints, but was very broadminded about external peculiarities and objective towards his opponents. He sought his field of labor most especially in the practical promotion of the moral life through the Church. In the pursuit of this end, as one of the most successful ministers known to history, he placed his services at the disposal of the Parliamentary Government, of Cromwell, and of the Restoration, until he retired, from office under the last, before St. Bartholomew's day. His Christian Directory is the most compendium of Puritan ethics, and is c adjusted to the practical experiences of his of his own ministerial activity. In comparison we shall make use of Spener's *Theologische Bedenken,* as representative of German Pietism, Barclay's *Apology* for the Quakers and some other representatives of ascetic ethics, which, however, in the interest of space, will be limited as far as possible.

Now, in glancing at Baxter's *Saints' Everlasting Rest*, or his *Christian Directory*, or similar works of others, one is struck at first glance by the emphasis placed, in the discussion of wealth and its acquisition, on the ebionitic elements of the New testament. Wealth as such is a great danger; its temptations never end and its pursuit[N] is not only senseless as compared with the dominating importance of the Kingdom of God, but it is morally suspect. Here asceticism seems to have turned much more sharply against the acquisition of earthly goods than it did in Calvin, who saw no hindrance to the effectiveness of the clergy in their wealth, but rather a thoroughly desirable enhancement of their prestige. Hence he permitted them to employ their means profitably. Examples of the condemnation of the pursuit of money and goods may be gathered without end from Puritan writings, and may be contrasted with the late mediaeval ethical literature, which was much more open-minded on this point.

Moreover, these doubts were meant with perfect seriousness; only it is necessary to examine them somewhat more closely in order to understand their true ethical significance and implications. The real moral objection is to relaxation in the security of possession, the enjoyment of wealth with the consequence of idleness and the temptations of the flesh, above all of distraction from the pursuit of a righteous life. In fact, it is only because possession involves this danger of relaxation that it is objectionable at all. For the saints' everlasting rest is in the next world; on earth man must, to be certain of his state of grace, "do the works of him who sent him, as long as it is yet day." Not leisure and enjoyment, but only activity serves to increase the glory of God, according to the definite manifestations of His will.

Waste of time is thus the first and in principle the deadliest of sins. The span of human life is infinitely short and precious to make sure of one's own election. Loss of time through sociability, idle talk,º luxury," even more sleep than is necessary for health, six to at most eight hours, is worthy of absolute moral condemnation. It does not yet hold, with Franklin, that time is money, but the proposition is true in a certain spiritual sense. It is infinitely valuable because every hour lost is lost to labor for the glory of God. Thus inactive contemplation is also valueless, or even directly reprehensible if it is at the expense of one's daily work. For it is less pleasing to God than the active performance of His will in a calling. Besides, Sunday is provided for that, and, according to Baxter, it is always those who are not diligent in their callings who have no time for God when the occasion demands it.

Accordingly, Baxter's principal work is dominated by the continually repeated, often almost passionate preaching of hard, continuous bodily or mental labor. It is due to a combination of two different motives.[66] Labor is, on the one hand, an approved ascetic technique, as it always has been in the Western Church, in sharp contrast not only to the Orient but to almost all monastic rules the world over. It is in particular the specific defense against all those temptations which Puritanism united under the name of the unclean life, whose role for it was by no means small. The sexual asceticism of Puritanism differs only in degree, not in fundamental principle, from that of monasticism; and on account of the Puritan conception of marriage, its practical influence is more far reaching than that of the latter. For sexual intercourse is permitted, even within marriage, only as the means willed by God for the increase of His glory according to the commandment, "Be fruitful and multiply." Along with a moderate vegetable diet and cold baths, the same prescription is given for all sexual temptations as is used against religious doubts and a sense of moral unworthiness: "Work hard in your calling." But the most important thing was that even beyond that labor came to

---

[66] That the peculiar ethical valuation of labor and its dignity was not originally a Christian idea nor even peculiar to Christianity has recently again been strongly emphasized by Harnack.

he considered in itself the end of life, ordained as such by God. St. Paul's "He who will not work shall not eat" holds unconditionally for everyone. Unwillingness to work is symptomatic of the lack of grace.

Here the difference from the medieval view-point becomes quite evident. Thomas Aquinas also gave an interpretation of that statement of St. Paul. But for him labor is only necessary *naturali ratione* for the maintenance of individual and community. Where this end is achieved, the precept ceases to have any meaning. Moreover, it holds only for the race, not for every individual. It does not apply to anyone who can live without labor on his possessions, and of course contemplation, as a spiritual form of action in the Kingdom of God, takes precedence over the commandment in its literal sense. Moreover, for the popular theology of the time, the highest form of monastic productivity lay in the increase of the *Thesaurus ecclesiae* through prayer and chant.

Now only do these exceptions to the duty to labor naturally no longer hold for Baxter, but he holds most emphatically that wealth does not exempt anyone from the unconditional command. Even the wealthy shall not cat without working, for even though they do not need to labor to support their own needs, there is God's commandment which they, like the poor, must obey. For everyone without exception God's Providence has prepared a calling, which he should profess and in which he should labor. And this calling is not, as it was for the Lutheran,[67] a fate to which he must submit and which he must make the best of, but God's commandment to the individual to work for the divine glory. This seemingly subtle difference had far-reaching psychological consequences, and became connected with a further development of the providential interpretation of the economic order which had begun in scholasticism.

The phenomenon of the division of labor and occupations in society had, among others, been interpreted by Thomas Aquinas, to whom we may most conveniently refer, as a direct consequence of the divine scheme of things. But the places assigned to each man in

---

[67] Including Pietism. Whenever a question of change of calling arises, Spener takes the attitude that after a certain calling has once been entered upon, it is a duty of obedience to Providence to remain and acquiesce in it.

this cosmos follow *ex causis naturalibus* and are fortuitous (contingent in the Scholastic terminology). The differentiation of men into the classes and occupations established through historical development became for Luther, as we have seen, a direct result of the divine will. The perseverance of the individual in the place and within the limits which God had assigned to him was a religious duty. This was the more certainly the consequence since the relations of Lutheranism to the world were in general uncertain from the beginning and remained so. Ethical principles for the reform of the world could not be found in Luther's realm of ideas; in fact it never quite freed itself from Pauline indifference. Hence the world had to be accepted as it was, and this alone could be made a religious duty.

But in the Puritan view, the providential character of the play of private economic interests takes on a somewhat different emphasis. True to the Puritan tendency to pragmatic interpretations, the providential purpose of the division of labor is to be known by its fruits. On this point Baxter expresses himself in terms which more than once directly recall Adam Smith's well-known apotheosis of the division of labor. The specialization of occupations leads, since it makes the development of skill possible, to a quantitative and qualitative improvement in production, and thus serves the common good, which is identical with the good of the greatest possible number. So far, the motivation is purely utilitarian, and is closely related to the customary view-point of much of the secular literature of the time.[r]

But the characteristic Puritan element appears when Baxter sets at the head of his discussion the statement that "outside of a well-marked calling the accomplishments of a man are only casual and irregular, and he spends more time in idleness than at work", and when he concludes it as follows: "and he (the specialized worker) will carry out his work in order while another remains in constant confusion, and his business knows neither time nor place . . . therefore is a certain calling the best for everyone." Irregular work, which the ordinary laborer is often forced to accept, is often unavoidable, but always an unwelcome state of transition. A man without a calling thus lacks the systematic, methodical character which is, as we have seen, demanded by worldly asceticism.

The Quaker ethic also holds that a man's life in his calling is an exercise in ascetic virtue, a proof of his state of grace through his conscientiousness, which is expressed in the care and method with which he pursues his calling. What God demands is not labor in itself, but rational labor in a calling. In the Puritan concept of the calling the emphasis is always placed on this methodical character of worldly asceticism, not, as with Luther, on the acceptance of the lot which God has irretrievably assigned to man.

Hence the question whether anyone may combine several callings is answered in the affirmative, if it is useful for the common good or one's own,[68] and not injurious to anyone, and if it does not lead to unfaithfulness in one of the callings. Even a change of calling is by no means regarded as objectionable, if it is not thoughtless and is made for the purpose of pursuing a calling more pleasing to God, which means, on general principles, one more useful.

It is true that the usefulness of a calling, and thus its favor in the sight of God, is measured primarily in moral terms, and thus in terms of the importance of the goods produced in it for the community. But a further, and, above all, in practice the most important, criterion is found in private profitableness. For if that God, whose hand the Puritan sees in all the occurrences of life, shows one of His elect a chance of profit, he must do it with a purpose. Hence the faithful Christian must follow the call by taking advantage of the opportunity. "If God show you a way in which you may lawfully get more than in another way (without wrong to your soul or to any other), if you refuse this, and choose the less gainful way, you cross one of the ends of your calling, and you refuse to be God's steward, and to accept His gifts and use them for Him, when He requireth it: you may labor to be rich for God, though not for the flesh and sin."

Wealth is thus bad ethically only in so far as it is a temptation to idleness and sinful enjoyment of life, and its acquisition is bad only when it is with the purpose of later living merrily and without care.

---

[68] For, as is often pointed out in the Puritan literature, God never commanded "love thy neighbor more than thyself", but only as thyself. Hence self-regard is also a duty. For instance, a man who can make better use of his possessions, to the greater glory of God, than his neighbor, is not obliged by the duty of brotherly love to part with them.

But as a performance of duty in a calling it is not only morally permissible, but actually enjoined. The parable of the servant who was rejected because he did not increase the talent which was entrusted to him seemed to say so directly. To wish to be poor was, it was often argued, the same as wishing to be unhealthy;[Q] it is objectionable as a glorification of works and derogatory to the glory of God. Especially begging, on the part of one able to work, is not only the sin of slothfulness, but a violation of the duty of brotherly love according to the Apostle's own word.

The emphasis on the ascetic importance of a fixed calling provided an ethical justification of the modern specialized division of labor. In a similar way the providential interpretation of profit-making justified the activities of the business man.[69] The superior indulgence of the seigneur and the parvenu ostentation of the nouveau riche are equally detestable to asceticism.

But, on the other hand, it has the highest ethical appreciation of the sober, middle-class, self-made Man. "God blesseth His trade" is a stock remark about those good men who had successfully followed the divine hints. The whole power of the God of the Old Testament, who rewards His people for their obedience in this life, necessarily exercised a similar influence on the Puritan who, following Baxter's advice, compared his own state of grace with that of the heroes of the Bible, and in the process interpreted the statements of the Scriptures as the articles of a book of statutes.

Of course, the words of the Old Testament were not entirely without ambiguity. We have seen that Luther first used the concept of the calling in the secular sense in translating a passage from Jesus Sirach. But the book of Jesus Sirach belongs, with the whole atmosphere expressed in it, to those parts of the broadened Old Testament with distinctly traditionalistic tendency, in spite of Hellenistic influences. It is characteristic that down to the present day this book seems to enjoy a special favor among Lutheran German peasants just as the Lutheran influence in large sections of German Pietism has been expressed by a preference for Jesus Sirach.

---

[69] The President of the Baptist Union of Great Britain and Ireland, G. White, said emphatically in his inaugural address before the assembly in London in 1903: "The best men on the roll of our Puritan Churches were men of affairs, who believed that religion should permeate the whole of life."

The Puritans repudiated the Apocrypha as not inspired, consistently with their sharp distinction between things divine and things of the flesh. But among the canonical books that of Job had all the more influence. On the one hand it contained a grand conception of the absolute sovereign majesty, of God, beyond all human comprehension, which was closely related to that of Calvinism. With that, on the other hand, it combined the certainty which, though incidental for Calvin, came to be of great importance for Puritanism, that God would bless His own in this life — in the book of Job only — and also in the material sense. The Oriental quietism, which appears in several of the finest verses of the Psalms and in the Proverbs, was interpreted away, just as Baxter did with the traditionalistic tinge of the passage in the 1st Epistle to the Corinthians, so important for the idea of the calling.

But all the more emphasis was placed on those parts of the Old Testament which praise formal legality as a sign of conduct pleasing to God. They held the theory that the Mosaic Law had only lost its validity through Christ in so far as it contained ceremonial or purely historical precepts applying only to the Jewish people, but that otherwise it had always been valid as an expression of the natural law, and must hence be retained. This made it possible, on the one hand, to eliminate elements which could not be reconciled with modern life. But still, through its numerous related features, Old Testament morality was able to give a powerful impetus to that spirit of self-righteous and sober legality which was so characteristic of the worldly asceticism of this form of Protestantism."

Thus when authors, as was the case with several contemporaries as well as later writers, characterize the basic ethical tendency of Puritanism, especially in England, as English Hebrews they are, correctly understood, not wrong. It is necessary, however, not to think of Palestinian Judaism at the time of the writing of the Scriptures, but of Judaism as it became under the influence of many centuries of formalistic, legalistic, and Talmudic education. Even then one must be very careful in drawing parallels. The general tendency of the older Judaism toward a naïve acceptance of life as such was far removed from the special characteristics of Puritanism. It was, however, just as far — and this ought not to be overlooked — from the economic ethics of mediaeval and modern Judaism, in the traits which determined the positions of both in the development of the capitalistic ethos. The Jews stood on the side of the politically and speculatively oriented adventurous capitalism; their ethos was, in a word, that of pariah-capitalism. But Puritanism carried the ethos of the rational organization of capital and labor. It took over from the Jewish ethic only what was adapted to this purpose.

To analyze the effects on the character of peoples of the penetration of life with Old Testament norms — a tempting task which, however, has not yet satisfactorily been done even for Judaism — would be impossible within the limits of this sketch. In addition to the relationships already pointed out, it is important for the general inner attitude of the Puritans, above all, that the belief that they were God's chosen people saw in them a great renaissance. Even the kindly Baxter thanked God that he was born in England, and thus in the true Church, and nowhere else. This thankfulness for one's own perfection by the grace of God penetrated the attitude toward life of the Puritan middle class, and played its part in developing that formalistic, hard, correct character which was peculiar to the men of that heroic age of capitalism.

Let us now try to clarify the points in which the Puritan idea of the calling and the premium it placed upon ascetic conduct was bound directly to influence the development of a capitalistic way of life. As we have seen, this asceticism turned with all its force against one thing: the spontaneous enjoyment of life and all it had to offer. This is perhaps most characteristically brought out in the struggle over the Book of Sports which James I and Charles I made into law expressly as a means of counteracting Puritanism, and which the latter ordered to be read from all the pulpits. The fanatical opposition of the Puritans to the ordinances of the King, permitting certain popular amusements on Sunday outside of Church hours by law, was not only explained by the disturbance of the Sabbath rest, but also by resentment against the intentional diversion from the ordered life of the saint, which it caused. And, on his side, the King's threats of severe punishment for every attack on the legality of those sports were motivated by his purpose of breaking the anti-authoritarian ascetic tendency of Puritanism, which was so dangerous to the State. The feudal and monarchical forces protected the pleasure seekers against the rising middle-class morality and the anti-authoritarian ascetic conventicles, just as today capitalistic society tends to protect those willing to work against the class morality of the proletariat and the anti-authoritarian trade union.

As against this the Puritans upheld their decisive characteristic, the principle of ascetic conduct. For otherwise the Puritan aversion to sport, even for the Quakers, was by no means simply one of principle. Sport was accepted if it served a rational purpose, that of recreation necessary for physical efficiency. But as a means for the spontaneous expression of undisciplined impulses, it was under suspicion; and in so far as it became purely a means of enjoyment, or awakened pride, raw instincts or the irrational gambling instinct, it was of course strictly condemned. Impulsive enjoyment of life, which leads away both from work in a calling and from religion, was as such the enemy of rational asceticism, whether in the form of seigneurial sports, or the enjoyment of the dance-hall or the public–house of the common man.

Its attitude was thus suspicious and often hostile to the aspects of culture without any immediate religious value. It is not, however, true that the ideals of Puritanism implied a solemn, narrow-minded contempt of culture. Quite the contrary is the case at least for science, with the exception of the hatred of Scholasticism. Moreover, the great men of the Puritan movement were thoroughly steeped in the culture of the Renaissance. The sermons of the Presbyterian divines abound with classical allusions and even the Radicals, although they objected to it, were not ashamed to display that kind of learning in theological polemics. Perhaps no country, was ever so full of graduates as New England in the first generation of its existence. The satire of their opponents, such as, for instance, Butler's *Hudibras*, also attacks primarily the pedantry and highly trained dialectics of the Puritans. This is partially due to the religious valuation of knowledge which followed from their attitude to the Catholic *fides implicita*.

But the situation is quite different when one looks at non-scientific literature and especially the fine arts. Here asceticism descended like a frost on the life of "Merrie old England." And not only worldly merriment felt its effect. The Puritan's ferocious hatred of everything which smacked of superstition, of all survivals of magical or sacramental salvation, applied to the Christmas festivities and the May Pole and all spontaneous religious art. That there was room in Holland for a great, often uncouthly realistic art proves only how far from completely the authoritarian moral discipline of that country was able to counteract the influence of the court and the regents (a class of *rentiers*), and also the joy in life of the parvenu bourgeoisie, after the short supremacy of the Calvinistic theocracy had been transformed into a moderate national Church, and with it Calvinism had perceptibly lost in its power of ascetic influence.

The theatre was obnoxious to the Puritans, and with the strict exclusion of the erotic and of nudity from the realm of toleration, a radical view of either literature or art could not exist. The conceptions of idle talk, of superfluities, and of vain ostentation, all designations of an irrational attitude without objective purpose, thus not ascetic, and especially not serving the glory of God, but of man, were always at hand to serve in deciding in favor of sober utility as against any artistic tendencies. This was especially true in the case of decoration of the person, for instance clothing. That powerful tendency toward uniformity of life, which today so immensely aids the capitalistic interest in the standardization of production," had its ideal foundations in the repudiation of all idolatry of the flesh.[70]

Of course we must not forget that Puritanism included a world of contradictions, and that the instinctive sense of eternal greatness in art was certainly stronger among its leaders than in the atmosphere of the Cavaliers.[71] Moreover, a unique genius like Rembrandt, however little his conduct may have been acceptable to God in the eyes of the Puritans, was very strongly influenced in the character of his work by his religious environment. But that does not alter the picture as a whole. In so far as the development of the Puritan tradition could, and in part did, lead to a powerful spiritualization of personality, it was a decided benefit to literature. But for the most part that benefit only accrued to later generations.

---

[70] Again and again we come back to this attitude. It explains statements like the following: "Every penny which is paid upon yourselves and children and friends must be done as by God's own appointment and to serve and please Him. Watch narrowly, or else that thievish, carnal self will leave God nothing."

[71] Quite rightly it is customary to recall that Cromwell saved Raphael's drawings and Mantegna's *Triumph of Cæsar* from destruction, while Charles II tried to sell them.

Although we cannot here enter upon a discussion of the influence of Puritanism in all these directions, we should call attention to the fact that the toleration of pleasure in cultural goods, which contributed to purely aesthetic or athletic enjoyment, certainly always ran up against one characteristic limitation: they must not cost anything. Man is only a trustee of the goods which "have come to him through God's grace. He must, like the servant in the parable, give an account of every penny entrusted to him, and it is at least hazardous to spend any of it for a purpose which does not serve the glory of God but only one's own enjoyment. What person, who keeps his eyes open, has not met representatives of this viewpoint even in the present?[R] The idea of a man's duty to his possessions, to which he subordinates himself as an obedient steward, or even as an acquisitive machine, bears with chilling weight J. on his life. The greater the possessions the heavier, if the ascetic attitude toward life stands the test, the feeling of responsibility for them, for holding them undiminished for the glory of God and increasing them by restless effort. The origin of this type of life also extends in certain roots, like so many aspects of the spirit of capitalism, back into the Middle Ages. But it was in the ethic of ascetic Protestantism that it first r found a consistent ethical foundation. Its significance for the development of capitalism is obvious.

This worldly Protestant asceticism, as we may recapitulate up to this point, acted powerfully against the spontaneous enjoyment of possessions; it restricted consumption, especially of luxuries. On the other hand, it had the psychological effect of freeing the acquisition of goods from the inhibitions of traditionalistic ethics. It broke the bonds of the impulse of acquisition in that it not only legalized it, but (in the sense discussed) looked upon it as directly willed by God. The campaign against the temptations of the flesh, and the dependence on external things, was, as besides the Puritans the great Quaker apologist Barclay expressly says, not a struggle against the rational acquisition, but against the irrational use of wealth.

But this irrational use was exemplified in the outward forms of luxury which their code condemned as idolatry of the flesh, however natural they had appeared to the feudal mind. On the other hand, they approved the rational and utilitarian uses of wealth which were willed by God for the needs of the individual and the community. They did not wish to impose mortification on the man of wealth, but the use of his means for necessary and practical things. The idea of comfort characteristically limits the extent of ethically permissible expenditures. It is naturally no accident that the development of a manner of living consistent with that idea may be observed earliest and most clearly among the most consistent representatives of this whole attitude toward life. Over against the glitter and ostentation of feudal magnificence which, resting on an unsound economic basis, prefers a sordid elegance to a sober simplicity, they set the clean and solid comfort of the middle-class home as an ideal."

On the side of the production of private wealth, asceticism condemned both dishonesty and impulsive avarice. What was condemned as covetousness, Mammonism, etc., was the pursuit of riches for their own sake. For wealth in itself was a temptation. But here asceticism was the power "which ever seeks the good but ever creates evil" what was evil in its sense was possession and its temptations. For, in conformity with the Old Testament and in analogy to the ethical valuation of good works, asceticism looked upon the pursuit of wealth as an end in itself as highly reprehensible; but the attainment of it as a fruit of labor in a calling was a sign of God's blessing. And even more important: the religious valuation of restless, continuous, systematic work in a worldly calling, a the highest means to asceticism, and at the same time the surest and most evident proof of rebirth and genuine faith, must have been the most powerful conceivable lever for the expansion of that attitude toward life which we have here called the spirit of capitalism.

When the limitation of consumption is combined with this release of acquisitive activity, the inevitable practical result is obvious: accumulation of capital through ascetic compulsion to save. The restraints which were imposed upon the consumption of wealth naturally served to increase it by making possible the productive investment of capital. How strong this influence was is not, unfortunately, susceptible of exact statistical demonstration. In New England the connection is so evident that it did not escape the eye of so discerning a historian as Doyle. But also in Holland, which was really only dominated by strict Calvinism for seven years, the greater simplicity of life in the more seriously religious circles, in combination with great wealth, led to an excessive propensity to accumulation.

That, furthermore, the tendency which has existed everywhere and at all times, being quite strong in Germany today, for middle-class fortunes to be absorbed into the nobility, was necessarily checked by the Puritan antipathy to the feudal way of life, is evident. English Mercantilist writers of the seventeenth century attributed the superiority of Dutch capital to English to the circumstance that newly acquired wealth there did not regularly seek investment in land. Also, since it is not simply a question of the purchase of land, it did not there seek to transfer itself to feudal habits of life, and thereby to remove itself from the possibility of capitalistic investment." The high esteem for agriculture as a peculiarly important branch of activity, also especially consistent with piety, which the Puritans shared, applied (for instance in Baxter) not to the landlord, but to the yeoman and farmer, in the eighteenth century not to the squire, but the rational cultivator.[72] Through the whole of English society in the time since the seventeenth century goes the conflict between the squirearchy, the representatives of "merrie old England", and the Puritan circles of widely varying social influence. Both elements, that of an unspoiled naïve joy of life, and of a strictly regulated, reserved self-control, and conventional ethical conduct are even today combined to form the English national character. Similarly, the early history of the North American Colonies is dominated by the sharp contrast of the adventurers, who wanted to set up plantations with the labor of indentured servants, and live as feudal lords, and the specifically middle-class outlook of the Puritans.

As far as the influence of the Puritan outlook extended, under all circumstances — and this is, of course, much more important than the mere encouragement of capital accumulation — it favored the development of a rational bourgeois economic life; it was the most important, and above all the only consistent influence in the

---

[72] Upon the strong movement for bourgeois capital to buy English landed estates followed the great period of prosperity of English agriculture.

development of that life. It stood at the cradle of the modern economic man.

To be sure, these Puritanical ideals tended to give way under excessive pressure from the temptations of wealth, as the Puritans themselves knew very well. With great regularity we find the most genuine adherents of Puritanism among the classes which were rising from a lowly status, the small bourgeois and farmers, while the *beati possidentes*, even among Quakers, are often found tending to repudiate the old ideals.[73] It was the same fate which again and again befell the predecessor of this worldly asceticism, the monastic asceticism of the Middle Ages. In the latter case, when rational economic activity had worked out its full effects by strict regulation of conduct and limitation of consumption, the wealth accumulated either succumbed directly to the nobility, as in the time before the Reformation, or monastic discipline threatened to break down, and one of the numerous reformations became necessary.

In fact the whole history of monasticism is in a certain sense the history of a continual struggle with the problem of the secularizing influence of wealth. The same is true on a grand scale of the worldly asceticism of Puritanism. The great revival of Methodism, which preceded the expansion of English industry toward the end of the eighteenth century, may well be compared with such a monastic reform. We may hence quote here a passage from John Wesley himself which might well serve as a motto for everything which has been said above. For it shows that the leaders of these ascetic movements understood the seemingly paradoxical relationships which we have here analyzed perfectly well, and in the same sense that we have given them.[s] He wrote:

"I fear, wherever riches have increased, the essence of religion has decreased in the same proportion. Therefore I do not see how it is possible, in the nature of things, for any revival of true religion to continue long. For religion must necessarily produce both industry and frugality, and these cannot but produce riches. But as riches increase, so will pride, anger, and love of the world in all its branches. How then is it possible that Methodism, that is, a religion

---

[73] On the way in which this was expressed in the politics of Pennsylvania in the eighteenth century, especially during the War of Independence.

of the heart, though it flourishes now as a green bay tree, should continue in this state? For the Methodists in every place grow diligent and frugal; consequently they increase in goods. Hence they proportionately increase in pride, in anger, in the desire of the flesh, the desire of the eyes, and the pride of life. So, although the form of religion remains, the spirit is swiftly vanishing away. Is there no way to prevent this continual decay of pure religion? We ought not to prevent people from being diligent and frugal; *we must exhort all Christians to gain all they can, and to save all they can; that is, in effect, to grow rich.*"[74]

There follows the advice that those who gain all they can and save all they can should also give all they can, so that they will grow in grace and lay up a treasure in heaven. It is clear that Wesley here expresses, even in detail, just what we have been trying to point out.

As Wesley here says, the full economic effect of those great religious movements, whose significance for economic development lay above all in their ascetic educative influence, generally came only after the peak of the purely religious enthusiasm was past. Then the intensity of the search for the Kingdom of God commenced gradually to pass over into sober economic virtue; the religious roots died out slowly, giving way to utilitarian worldliness. Then, as Dowden puts it, as in *Robinson Crusoe*, the isolated economic man who carries on missionary activities on the side[75] takes the place of the lonely spiritual search for the Kingdom of Heaven of Bunyan's pilgrim, hurrying through the market-place of Vanity.

When later the principle "to make the most of both worlds" became dominant in the end, as Dowden has remarked, a good conscience simply became one of the means of enjoying a comfortable bourgeois life, as is well expressed in the German proverb about the soft pillow. What the great religious epoch of the seventeenth century bequeathed to its utilitarian successor was, however, above all an amazingly good, we may even say a pharisaically good, conscience in the acquisition of money, so long

---

[74] That exactly the same things were obvious to the Puritans of the classical era cannot perhaps be more clearly shown than by the fact that in Bunyan Mr. Money-Love argues that one may become religious in order to get rich, for instance to attract customers. For why one has become religious makes no difference.

[75] Defoe was a zealous Nonconformist.

as it took place legally. Every trace of the *deplacere vix potest* has disappeared."

A specifically bourgeois economic ethic had grown up. With the consciousness of standing in the fullness of God's grace and being visibly blessed by Him, the bourgeois business man, as long as he remained within the bounds of formal correctness, as long as his moral conduct was spotless and the use to which he put his wealth was not objectionable, could follow his pecuniary interests as he would and feel that he was fulfilling a duty in doing so. The power of religious asceticism provided him in addition with sober, conscientious, and unusually industrious workmen, who clung to their work as to a life purpose willed by God.

Finally, it gave him the comforting assurance that the unequal distribution of the goods of this world was a special dispensation of Divine Providence, which in these differences, as in particular grace, pursued secret ends unknown to men.[76] Calvin himself had made the much-quoted statement that only when the people, *i.e.* the mass of laborers and craftsmen, were poor did they remain obedient to God.[77] In the Netherlands (Pieter de la Court and others), that had been secularized to the effect that the mass of men only labor when necessity forces them to do so. This formulation of a leading idea of capitalistic economy later entered into the current theories of the productivity of low wages. Here also, with the dying out of the religious root, the utilitarian interpretation crept in unnoticed, in the line of development which we have again and again observed.

Mediaeval ethics not only tolerated begging but actually glorified it in the mendicant orders. Even secular beggars, since they gave the person of means opportunity for good works through giving alms, were sometimes considered an estate and treated as such. Even the Anglican social ethic of the Stuarts was very close to this attitude. It remained for Puritan Asceticism to take part in the severe English Poor Relief Legislation which fundamentally changed the situation.

---

[76] The analogy between the unjust (according to human standards) predestination of only a few and the equally unjust, but equally divinely ordained, distribution of wealth was too obvious to be escaped. Furthermore, as for Baxter: poverty is very often a symptom of sinful slothfulness.

[77] Thomas Adams thinks that God probably allows so many people to remain poor because He knows that they would not be able to withstand the temptations that go with wealth. For wealth all too often draws men away from religion.

And it could do that because the Protestant sects and the strict Puritan communities actually did not know any begging in their own midst.

On the other hand, seen from the side of the workers, the Zinzendorf branch of Pietism, for instance, glorified the loyal worker who did not seek acquisition, but lived according to the apostolic model, and was thus endowed with the charisma of the disciples.[78] Similar ideas had originally been prevalent among the Baptists

Now naturally the whole ascetic literature of almost all denominations is saturated with the idea that faithful labor, even at low wages, on the part of those whom life offers no other opportunities, is highly pleasing to God. In this respect Protestant Asceticism added in itself nothing new. But it not only deepened this idea most powerfully, it also created the force which was alone decisive for its effectiveness: the psychological sanction of it through the conception of this labor as a calling, as the best, often in the last analysis the only means of attaining certainty of grace. And on the other hand it legalized the exploitation of this specific willingness to work, in that it also interpreted the employer's business activity as a calling.[79] It is obvious how powerfully the exclusive search for the Kingdom of God only through the fulfillment of duty in the calling, and the strict asceticism which Church discipline naturally imposed, especially on the propertyless classes, was bound to affect the productivity of labor in the capitalistic sense of the word. The treatment of labor as a calling became as characteristic of the modern worker as the corresponding attitude toward acquisition of the business man. It was a perception of this situation, new at his time, which caused so able an observer as Sir William Petty to attribute the economic power of Holland in the seventeenth century to the fact that the very numerous dissenters in that country (Calvinists and Baptists) "are for the most part thinking, sober men, and such as believe that Labor and Industry is their duty towards God."

---

[78] Similar things were not lacking in England. There was, for example, that Pietism which, starting from Law's *Serious Call* (1728), preached poverty, chastity, and, originally, isolation from the world.

[79] Furthermore, one may well doubt to what extent the joy of the mediæval craftsman in his creation, which is so commonly appealed to, was effective as a psychological motive force. Nevertheless, there is undoubtedly something in that thesis.

Calvinism opposed organic social organization in the fiscal-monopolistic form which it assumed in Anglicanism under the Stuarts, especially in the conceptions of Laud, this alliance of Church and State with the monopolists on the basis of a Christian, social ethical foundation. Its leaders were universally among the most passionate opponents of this type of politically privileged commercial, putting-out, and colonial capitalism. Over against it they placed the individualistic motives of rational legal acquisition by virtue of one's own ability and initiative. And, while the politically privileged monopoly industries in England all disappeared in short order, this attitude played a large and decisive part in the development of the industries which grew up in spite of and against the authority of the State. The Puritans (Prynne, Parker) repudiated all connection with the large-scale capitalistic courtiers and projectors as an ethically suspicious class. On the other hand, they took pride in their own superior middle-class business morality, which formed the true reason for the persecutions to which they were subjected on the part of those circles. Defoe proposed to win the battle against dissent by boycotting bank credit and withdrawing deposits. The difference of the two types of capitalistic attitude went to a very large extent hand in hand with religious differences. The opponents of the Nonconformists, even in the eighteenth century, again and again ridiculed them for personifying the spirit of shopkeepers, and for having, ruined the ideals of old England. Here also lay the difference of the Puritan economic ethic from the Jewish; and contemporaries (Prynne) knew well that the former and not the latter was the bourgeois capitalistic ethic.

One of the fundamental elements of the spirit of modern capitalism, and not only of that but of all modern culture: rational conduct on the basis of the idea of the calling, was born — that is what this discussion has sought to demonstrate — from the spirit of Christian asceticism. One has only to reread the passage from Franklin, quoted at the beginning of this essay, in order to see that the essential elements of the attitude which was there called the spirit of capitalism are the same as what we have just shown to be the content of the Puritan worldly asceticism, only without the religious basis, which by Franklin's time bad died away. The idea that modern labor has an ascetic character is of course not new. Limitation to specialized work, with a renunciation of the Faustian universality of man which it involves, is a condition of any valuable work in the modern world; hence deeds and renunciation inevitably condition each other today. This fundamentally ascetic trait of middle-class life, if it attempts to be a way of life at all, and not simply the absence of any, was what Goethe wanted to teach, at the height of his wisdom, in the *Wanderjahren*, and in the end which he gave to the life of his Faust. For him the realization meant a renunciation, a departure from an age of full and beautiful humanity, which can no more be repeated in the course of our cultural development than can the flower of the Athenian culture of antiquity.

The Puritan wanted to work in a calling; we are forced to do so. For when asceticism was carried out of monastic cells into everyday life, and began to dominate worldly morality, it did its part in building the tremendous cosmos of the modern economic order. This order is now bound to the technical and economic conditions of machine production which today determine the lives of all the individuals who are born into this mechanism, not only those directly concerned with economic acquisition, with irresistible force. Perhaps it will so determine them until the last ton of fossilized coal is burnt. In Baxter's view tile care for external goods should only lie on the shoulders of the "saint like a light cloak, which can be thrown aside at any moment." But fate decreed that the cloak should become an iron cage.

Since asceticism undertook to remodel the world and to work out its ideals in the world, material goods have gained an increasing and finally an inexorable power over the lives of men as at no previous period in history. Today the spirit of religious asceticism—whether finally, who knows?—has escaped from the cage. But victorious capitalism, since it rests on mechanical foundations, needs its support no longer. The rosy blush of its laughing heir, the Enlightenment, seems also to be irretrievably fading, and the idea of duty in one's calling prowls about in our lives like the ghost of dead religious beliefs. Where the fulfillment of the calling cannot directly be related to the highest spiritual and cultural values, or when, on the other hand, it need not be felt simply as economic compulsion, the individual generally abandons the attempt to justify it at all. In the field of its highest development, in the United States, the pursuit of wealth, stripped of its religious and ethical meaning, tends to become associated with purely mundane passions, which often actually give it the character of sport.

No one knows who will live in this cage in the future, or whether at the end of this tremendous development, entirely new prophets will arise, or there will be a great rebirth of old ideas and ideals, or, if neither, mechanized petrification, embellished with a sort of convulsive self-importance. For of the fast stage of this cultural development, it might well be truly said: "Specialists without spirit, sensualists without heart; this nullity imagines that it has attained a level of civilization never before achieved."

But this brings us to the world of judgments of value and of faith, with which this purely historical discussion need not be burdened. The next task would be rather to show the significance of ascetic rationalism which has only been touched in the foregoing sketch for the content of practical social ethics, thus for the types of organization and the functions of social groups from the conventicle to the State. Then its relations to humanistic rationalism, its ideals of life and cultural influence; further to the development of philosophical and scientific empiricism, to technical development and to spiritual ideals would have to be analyzed. Then its historical development from the mediaeval beginnings of worldly asceticism to its dissolution into pure utilitarianism would have to be traced out through all the areas of ascetic religion. Only then could the quantitative cultural significance of ascetic Protestantism in its relation to the other plastic elements of modern culture be estimated.

Here we have only attempted to trace the fact and the direction of its influence to their motives in one, though a very important point. But it would also further be necessary to investigate how Protestant Asceticism was in turn influenced in its development and its character by the totality of social conditions, especially economic. The modern man is in general, even with the best will, unable to give religious ideas a significance for culture and national character which they deserve. But it is, of course, not my aim to substitute for a one-sided materialistic an equally one sided spiritualistic causal interpretation of culture and of history. Each is equally possible, but each, if it does not serve as the preparation, but as the conclusion of an investigation, accomplishes equally little in the interest of historical truth.[T]

Endnotes

A From the voluminous literature which has grown up around this essay I cite only the most comprehensive criticisms. (1) F. Rachfahl, "Kalvinismus und Kapitalismus", *Internationale Wochenschrift für Wissenschaft, Kunst und Technik* (1909), Nos. 39–43. In reply, my article: "Antikritisches zum Geist des Kapitalismus," *Archiv für Sozialwissenschaft und Sozialpolitik* (Tübingen), XX, 1910. Then Rachfahl's reply to that: "Nochmals Kalvinismus und Kapitalismus", 1910, Nos. 22–25, of the *Internationale Wochenschrift*. Finally my "Antikritisches Schlusswort", *Archiv*, XXXI. (Brentano, in the criticism presently to be referred to, evidently did not know of this last phase of the discussion, as he does not refer to it.) I have not incorporated anything in this edition from the somewhat unfruitful polemics against Rachfahl. He is an author whom I otherwise admire, but who has in this instance ventured into a field which he has not thoroughly mastered. I have only added a few supplementary references from my anti-critique, and have attempted, in new passages and footnotes, to make impossible any future misunderstanding. (2) W. Sombart, in his book *Der Bourgeois* (Munich and Leipzig, 1913, also translated into English under the title *The Quintessence of Capitalism*, London, 1915), to which I shall return in footnotes below, Finally (3) Lujo Brentano in Part II of the Appendix to his Munich address (in the Academy of Sciences, 1913) on *Die Anfänge des modernen Kapitalismus*, which was published in 1916. (Since Weber's death Brentano has somewhat expanded these essays and incorporated them into his recent book *Der wirtschaftende Mensch in der Geschichte.*—Translator's Note.) I shall also refer to this criticism in special footnotes in the proper places. I invite anyone who may be interested to convince himself by comparison that I have not in revision left out, changed the meaning of, weakened, or added materially different statements to, a single sentence of my essay which contained any essential point. There was no occasion to do so, and the development of my exposition will convince anyone who still doubts. The two latter writers engaged in a more bitter quarrel with each other than with me. Brentano's criticism of Sombart's book, *Die Juden und das Wirtschaftsleben*, I consider in many points well founded, but often very unjust, even apart from the fact that Brentano does not himself seem to understand the real essence of the problem of the Jews (which is entirely omitted from this essay, but will be dealt with later [in a later section of the *Religionssoziologie.*—Translator's Note]).

From theologians I have received numerous valuable suggestions in connection with this study. Its reception on their part has been in general friendly and impersonal, in spite of wide differences of opinion on particular points. This is the more welcome to me since I should not have wondered at a certain antipathy to the manner in which these matters must necessarily be treated here. What to a theologian is valuable in his religion cannot play a very large part in this study. We are concerned with what, from a religious point of view, are often quite superficial and unrefined aspects of religious life, but which, and precisely because they were superficial and unrefined, have often influenced outward behavior most profoundly.

Another book which, besides containing many other things, is a very welcome confirmation of and supplement to this essay in so far as it deals with our problem, is the important work of E. Troeltsch, *Die Soziallehren der christlichen Kirchen und Gruppen* (Tübingen, 1912). It deals with the history of the ethics of Western Christianity from a very comprehensive point of view of its own. I here refer the reader to it for general comparison instead of making repeated references to special points. The author is principally concerned with the doctrines of religion, while I am interested rather in their practical results.

[B] The exceptions are explained, not always, but frequently, by the fact that the religious leanings of the laboring force of an industry are naturally, in the first instance, determined by those of the locality in which the industry is situated, or from which its labor is drawn. This circumstance often alters the impression given at first glance by some statistics of religious adherence, for instance in the Rhine provinces. Furthermore, figures can naturally only be conclusive if individual specialized occupations are carefully distinguished in them. Otherwise very large employers may sometimes be grouped together with master craftsmen who work alone, under the category of "proprietors of enterprises." Above all, the fully developed capitalism of the present day, especially so far as the great unskilled lower strata of labor are concerned, has become independent of any influence which religion may have had in the past. I shall return to this point.

[c] I make use of this opportunity to insert a few anti-critical remarks in advance of the main argument. Sombart (*Bourgeois*) makes the untenable statement that this ethic of Franklin is a word-for-word repetition of some writings of that great and versatile genius of the Renaissance, Leon Battista Alberti, who besides theoretical treatises on Mathematics, Sculpture, Painting, Architecture, and Love (he was personally a woman-hater), wrote a work in four books on household management (*Della Famiglia*). (Unfortunately, I have not at the time of writing been able to procure the edition of Mancini, but only the older one of Bonucci.) The passage from Franklin is printed above word for word. Where then are corresponding passages to be found in Alberti's work, especially the maxim "time is money", which stands at the head, and the exhortations which follow it? The only passage which, so far as I know, bears the slightest resemblance to it is found towards the end of the first book of *Della Famiglia* (ed. Bonucci, II, p. 353), where Alberti speaks in very general terms of money as the *nervus rerum* of the household, which must hence be handled with special care, just as Cato spoke in *De Re Rustica*. To treat Alberti, who was very proud of his descent from one of the most distinguished cavalier families of Florence (*Nobilissimi Cavalieri, op. cit.*, pp. 213, 228, 247, etc.), as a man of mongrel blood who was filled with envy for the noble families because his illegitimate birth, which was not in the least socially disqualifying, excluded him as a bourgeois from association with the nobility, is

quite incorrect. It is true that the recommendation of large enterprises as alone worthy of a *nobile è onesta famiglia* and a *libero è nobile animo*, and as costing less labor is characteristic of Alberti (p. 209; compare *Del governo della Famiglia*, IV, p. 55, as well as p. 116 in the edition for the Pandolfini). Hence the best thing is a putting-out business for wool and silk. Also an ordered and painstaking regulation of his household, *i.e.* the limiting of expenditure to income. This is the *santa masserizia*, which is thus primarily a principle of maintenance, a given standard of life, and not of acquisition (as no one should have understood better than Sombart). Similarly, in the discussion of the nature of money, his concern is with the management of consumption funds (money or *possessioni*), not with that of capital; all that is clear from the expression of it which is put into the mouth of Gianozzo. He recommends, as protection against the uncertainty of *fortuna*, early habituation to continuous activity, which is also (pp. 73–4) alone healthy in the long run, *in cose magnifiche è ample*, and avoidance of laziness, which always endangers the maintenance of one's position in the world. Hence a careful study of a suitable trade in case of a change of fortune, but every *opera mercenaria* is unsuitable (*op. cit.*, I, p. 209). His idea of *tranquillita dell' animo* and his strong tendency toward the Epicurean (*vivere a sè stesso*, p. 262); especially his dislike of any office (p. 258) as a source of unrest, of making enemies, and of becoming involved in dishonourable dealings; the ideal of life in a country villa; his nourishment of vanity through the thought of his ancestors; and his treatment of the honour of the family (which on that account should keep its fortune together in the Florentine manner and not divide it up) as a decisive standard and ideal — all these things would in the eyes of every Puritan have been sinful idolatry of the flesh, and in those of Benjamin Franklin the expression of incomprehensible aristocratic nonsense. Note, further, the very high opinion of literary things (for the *industria* is applied principally to literary and scientific work), which is really most worthy of a man's efforts. And the expression of the *masserizia*, in the sense of "rational conduct of the household" as the means of living independently of others and avoiding destitution, is in general put only in the mouth of the illiterate Gianozzo as of equal value. Thus the origin of this concept –

Now compare all this with the ethic and manner of life of Benjamin Franklin, and especially of his Puritan ancestors; the works of the Renaissance *littérateur* addressing himself to the humanistic aristocracy, with Franklin's works addressed to the masses of the lower middle class (he especially mentions clerks) and with the tracts and sermons of the Puritans, in order to comprehend the depth of the difference. The economic rationalism of Alberti, everywhere supported by references to ancient authors, is most clearly related to the treatment of economic problems in the works of Xenophon (whom he did not know), of Cato, Varro, and Columella (all of whom he quotes), except that especially in Cato and Varro, *acquisition* as such stands in the foreground in a different way from that to be found in Alberti. Furthermore, the very occasional comments of Alberti on the use of the *fattori*, their division of labor and discipline, on the unreliability of the peasants, etc., really sound as if Cato's homely wisdom were taken from the field of the ancient slave-using household and applied to that of free labor in domestic industry and the metayer system. When Sombart (whose reference to the Stoic ethic is quite misleading) sees economic rationalism as "developed to its farthest conclusions" as early as Cato, he is, with a correct interpretation, not entirely wrong. It is possible to unite the *diligens pater familias* of the Romans with the ideal of the *massajo* of Alberti under the same category. It is above all characteristic for Cato that a landed estate is valued and judged as an object for the investment of consumption funds. The concept of *industria*, on the other hand, is differently coloured on account of Christian influence. And there is just the difference. In the conception of *industria*, which comes from monastic asceticism and which was developed by monastic writers, lies the seed of an *ethos* which was fully developed later in the Protestant worldly asceticism. Hence, as we shall often point out, the relationship of the two, which, however, is less close to the official Church doctrine of St. Thomas than to the Florentine and Siennese mendicant-moralists. In Cato and also in Alberti's own writings this *ethos* is lacking; for both it is a matter of worldly wisdom, not of ethic. In Franklin there is also a utilitarian strain. But the ethical quality of the sermon to young business men is impossible to mistake, and that is the characteristic thing. A lack of care in the handling of money means to him that one so to speak murders capital embryos, and hence it is an ethical defect.

An inner relationship of the two (Alberti and Franklin) exists in fact only in so far as Alberti, whom Sombart calls pious, but who actually, although he took the sacraments and held a Roman benefice, like so many humanists, did not himself (except for two quite colorless passages) in any way make use of religious motives as a justification of the manner of life he recommended, had not yet, Franklin on the other hand no longer, related his recommendation of economy to religious conceptions. Utilitarianism, in Alberti's preference for wool and silk manufacture, also the mercantilist social utilitarianism "that many people should be given employment" (see Alberti, *op. cit.*, p. 292), is in this field at least formally the sole justification for the one as for the other. Alberti's discussions of this subject form an excellent example of the sort of economic rationalism which really existed as a reflection of economic conditions, in the work of authors interested purely in "the thing for its own sake" everywhere and at all times; in the Chinese classicism and in Greece and Rome no less than in the Renaissance and the age of the Enlightenment. There is no doubt that just as in ancient times with Cato, Varro, and Columella, also here with Alberti and others of the same type, especially in the doctrine of *industria*, a sort of economic rationality is highly developed. But how can anyone believe that such a literary *theory* could develop into a revolutionary force at all comparable to the way in which a religious belief was able to set the sanctions of salvation and damnation on the fulfillment of a particular (in this case methodically rationalized) manner of life? What, as compared with it, a really religiously oriented rationalization of conduct looks like, may be seen, outside of the Puritans of all denominations, in the cases of the

Jains, the Jews, certain ascetic sects of the Middle Ages, the Bohemian Brothers (an offshoot of the Hussite movement), the Skoptsi and Stundists in Russia, and numerous monastic orders, however much all these may differ from each other.

The essential point of the difference is (to anticipate) that an ethic based on religion places certain psychological sanctions (not of an economic character) on the maintenance of the attitude prescribed by it, sanctions which, so long as the religious belief remains alive, are highly effective, and which mere worldly wisdom like that of Alberti does not have at its disposal. Only in so far as these sanctions work, and, above all, in the direction in which they work, which is often very different from the doctrine of the theologians, does such an ethic gain an independent influence on the conduct of life and thus on the economic order. This is, to speak frankly, the point of this whole essay, which I had not expected to find so completely overlooked.

Later on I shall come to speak of the theological moralists of the late Middle Ages, who were relatively friendly to capital (especially Anthony of Florence and Bernhard of Siena), and whom Sombart has also seriously misinterpreted. In any case Alberti did not belong to that group. Only the concept of *industria* did he take from monastic lines of thought, no matter through what intermediate links. Alberti, Pandolfini, and their kind are representatives of that attitude which, in spite of all its outward obedience, was inwardly already emancipated from the tradition of the Church. With all its resemblance to the current Christian ethic, it was to a large extent of the antique pagan character, which Brentano thinks I have ignored in its significance for the development of modern economic thought (and also modern economic policy). That I do not deal with its influence here is quite true. It would be out of place in a study of the Protestant ethic and the spirit of capitalism. But, as will appear in a different connection, far from denying its significance, I have been and am for good reasons of the opinion that its sphere and direction of influence were entirely different from those of the Protestant ethic (of which the spiritual ancestry, of no small practical importance, lies in the sects and in the ethics of Wyclif and Hus). It was not the mode of life of the rising bourgeoisie which was influenced by this other attitude, but the policy of statesmen and princes; and these two partly, but by no means always, convergent lines of development should for purposes of analysis be kept perfectly distinct. So far as Franklin is concerned, his tracts of advice to business men, at present used for school reading in America, belong in fact to a category of works which have influenced practical life, far more than Alberti's large book, which hardly became known outside of learned circles. But I have expressly denoted him as a man who stood beyond the direct influence of the Puritan view of life, which had paled considerably in the meantime, just as the whole English enlightenment, the relations of which to Puritanism have often been set forth.

ᴰ This is perhaps the most appropriate place to make a few remarks concerning the essay of F. Keller, already referred to (volume 12 of the publications of the

Görres-Gesellschaft), and Sombart's observations (*Der Bourgeois*) in following it up, so far as they are relevant in the present context. That an author should criticize a study in which the canonical prohibition of interest (except in one incidental remark which has no connection with the general argument) is not even mentioned, on the assumption that this prohibition of interest, which has a parallel in almost every religious ethic in the world, is taken to be the decisive criterion of the difference between the Catholic and Protestant ethics, is almost inconceivable. One should really only criticize things which one has read, or the argument of which, if read, one has not already forgotten. The campaign against *usuraria pravitas* runs through both the Huguenot and the Dutch Church history of the sixteenth century; Lombards, *i.e.* bankers, were by virtue of that fact alone often excluded from communion (see Chap. 1, note 17). The more liberal attitude of Calvin (which did not, however, prevent the inclusion of regulations against usury in the first plan of the ordinances) did not gain a definite victory until Salmasius. Hence the difference did not lie at this point; quite the contrary. But still worse are the author's own arguments on this point. Compared to the works of Funck and other Catholic scholars (which he has not, in my opinion, taken as fully into consideration as they deserve), and the investigations of Endemann, which, however obsolete in certain points to-day, are still fundamental, they make a painful impression of superficiality. To be sure, Keller has abstained from such excesses as the remarks of Sombart (*Der Bourgeois*, p. 321) that one noticed how the "pious gentlemen" (Bernard of Siena and Anthony of Florence) "wished to excite the spirit of enterprise by every possible means", that is, since they, just like nearly everyone else concerned with the prohibition of interest, interpreted it in such a way as to exempt what we should call the productive investment of capital. That Sombart, on the one hand, places the Romans among the heroic peoples, and on the other, what is for his work as a whole an impossible contradiction, considers economic rationalism to have been developed to its final consequences in Cato (p. 267), may be mentioned by the way as a symptom that this is a book with a thesis in the worst sense.

He has also completely misrepresented the significance of the prohibition of interest. This cannot be set forth here in detail. At one time it was often exaggerated, then strongly underestimated, and now, in an era which produces Catholic millionaires as well as Protestant, has been turned upside down for apologetic purposes. As is well known, it was not, in spite of Biblical authority, abolished until the last century by order of the *Congregatio S. Officii*, and then only *temporum ratione habita* and indirectly, namely, by forbidding confessors to worry their charges by questions about *usuraria pravitas*, even though no claim to obedience was given up in case it should be restored. Anyone who has made a thorough study of the extremely complicated history of the doctrine cannot claim, considering the endless controversies over, for instance, the justification of the purchase of bonds, the discounting of notes and various other contracts (and above all considering the order of the *Congregatio S. Officii*, mentioned above, concerning a municipal loan), that the prohibition of interest was only intended to apply to emergency loans, nor that it had the intention of preserving capital, or that it was even an aid to capitalistic enterprise (p. 25). The truth is that the Church came to reconsider the prohibition of interest comparatively late. At the time when this happened the forms of purely business investment were not loans at fixed interest rate, but the *fœnus nauticum, commenda, societas maris,* and the *dare ad proficuum de mari* (a loan in which the shares of gain and loss were adjusted according to degrees of risk), and were, considering the character of the return on loans to productive enterprise, necessarily of that sort. These were not (or only according to a few rigorous canonists) held to fall under the ban, but when investment at a definite rate of interest and discounting became possible and customary, the first sort of loans also encountered very troublesome difficulties from the prohibition, which led to various drastic measures of the merchant guilds (black lists). But the treatment of usury on the part of the canonists was generally purely legal and formal, and was certainly free from any such tendency to protect capital as Keller ascribes to it. Finally, in so far as any attitude towards capitalism as such can be ascertained, the decisive factors were: on the one hand, a traditional, mostly inarticulate hostility towards the growing power of capital which was impersonal, and hence not readily amenable to ethical control (as it is still reflected in Luther's pronouncements about the Fuggers and about the banking business); on the other hand, the necessity of accommodation to practical needs. But we cannot discuss this, for, as has been said, the prohibition of usury and its fate can have at most a symptomatic significance for us, and that only to a limited degree.

The economic ethic of the Scotists, and especially of certain mendicant theologians of the fourteenth century, above all Bernhard of Siena and Anthony of Florence, that is monks with a specifically rational type of asceticism, undoubtedly deserves a separate treatment, and cannot be disposed of incidentally in our discussion. Otherwise I should be forced here, in reply to criticism, to anticipate what I have to say in my discussion of the economic ethics of Catholicism in its positive relations to capitalism. These authors attempt, and in that anticipate some of the Jesuits, to present the profit of the merchant as a reward for his *industria,* and thus ethically to justify it. (Of course, even Keller cannot claim more.)

The concept and the approval of *industria* come, of course, in the last analysis from monastic asceticism, probably also from the idea of *masserizia,* which Alberti, as he himself says through the mouth of Gianozzo, takes over from clerical sources. We shall later speak more fully of the sense in which the monastic ethics is a forerunner of the worldly ascetic denominations of Protestantism. In Greece, among the Cynics, as shown by late-Hellenic tombstone inscriptions, and, with an entirely different background, in Egypt, there were suggestions of similar ideas. But what is for us the most important thing is entirely lacking both here and in the case of Alberti. As we shall see later, the characteristic Protestant conception of the proof of one's own salvation, the *certitudo salutis* in a calling, provided the psychological sanctions which this religious belief put behind the *industria.* But that Catholicism could not supply, because its means to salvation were different. In effect these authors are concerned with an ethical doctrine, not with motives to practical action, dependent on the desire for salvation. Furthermore, they are, as is very easy to see, concerned with concessions to practical necessity, not, as was worldly asceticism, with deductions from fundamental religious postulates. (Incidentally, Anthony and Bernhard have long ago been better dealt with than by Keller.) And even these concessions have remained an object of controversy down to the present. Nevertheless the significance of these monastic ethical conceptions as symptoms is by no means small.

But the real roots of the religious ethics which led the way to the modern conception of a calling lay in the sects and the heterodox movements, above all in Wyclif; although Brodnitz (*Englische Wirtschaftsgeschichte*), who thinks his influence was so great that Puritanism found nothing left for it to do, greatly overestimates his significance. All that cannot be gone into here. For here we can only discuss incidentally whether and to what extent the Christian ethic of the Middle Ages had in fact already prepared the way for the spirit of capitalism.

E According to Richard Baxter everything is sinful which is contrary to the reason given by God as a norm of action. Not only passions which have a sinful content, but all feelings which are senseless and intemperate as such. They destroy the countenance and, as things of the flesh, prevent us from rationally directing all action and feeling to God, and thus insult Him. Compare what is said of the sinfulness of anger (*Christian Directory*, second edition, 1698, p. 285. Tauler is cited on p. 287). On the sinfulness of anxiety, *Ebenda*, I, p. 287. That it is idolatry if our appetite is made the "rule or measure of eating" is maintained very emphatically (*op. cit.*, I, pp. 310, 316, and elsewhere). In such discussions reference is made everywhere to the Proverbs and also to Plutarch's *De tranquilitate Animi*, and not seldom to ascetic writings of the Middle Ages: St. Bernard, Bonaventura, and others. The contrast to "who does not love wine, women, and song . . ." could hardly be more sharply drawn than by the extension of the idea of idolatry to all sensuous pleasures, so far as they are not justified by hygienic considerations, in which case they (like sport within these limits, but also other recreations) are permissible. See below (Chapter 5) for further discussion. Please note that the sources referred to here and elsewhere are neither dogmatic nor edifying works, but grew out of practical ministry, and thus give a good picture of the direction which its influence took.

F I should regret it if any evaluation of one or the other form of religion should be read into this discussion. We are not concerned with that here. It is only a question of the influence of certain things which, from a purely religious point of view, are perhaps incidental, but important for practical conduct.

G It is well known that this attitude made it possible for Pietism to be one of the main forces behind the idea of toleration. At this point we may insert a few remarks on that subject. In the West its historical origin, if we omit the humanistic indifference of the Enlightenment, which in itself has never had great practical influence, is to be found in the following principal sources: (1) Purely political expediency (type: William of Orange). (2) Mercantilism (especially clear for the City of Amsterdam, but also typical of numerous cities, landlords, and rulers who received the members of sects as valuable for economic progress). (3) The radical wing of Calvinism. Predestination made it fundamentally impossible for the State really to promote religion by intolerance. It could not thereby save a single soul. Only the idea of the glory of God gave the Church occasion to claim its help in the suppression of heresy. Now the greater the emphasis on the membership of the preacher, and all those that partook of the communion, in the elect, the more intolerable became the interference of the State in the appointment of the clergy.

For clerical positions were often granted as benefices to men from the universities only because of their theological training, though they might be personally unregenerate. In general, any interference in the affairs of the religious community by those in political power, whose conduct might often be unsatisfactory, was resented. Reformed Pietism strengthened this tendency by weakening the emphasis on doctrinal orthodoxy and by gradually undermining the principle of *extra ecclesiam nulla salus*.

Calvin had regarded the subjection of the damned to the divine supervision of the Church as alone consistent with the glory of God; in New England the attempt was made to constitute the Church as an aristocracy of proved saints. Even the radical Independents, however, repudiated every interference of temporal or any sort of hierarchical powers with the proof of salvation which was only possible within the individual community. The idea that the glory of God requires the subjection of the damned to the discipline of the Church was gradually superseded by the other idea, which was present from the beginning and became gradually more prominent, that it was an insult to His glory to partake of the Communion with one rejected by God. That necessarily led to voluntarism, for it led to the believers' Church the religious community which included only the twice-born. Calvinistic Baptism, to which, for instance, the leader of the Parliament of Saints Praise god Barebones belonged, drew the consequences of this line of thought with great emphasis. Cromwell's army upheld the liberty of conscience and the parliament of saints even advocated the separation of Church and State, because its members were good Pietists, thus on positive religious grounds. (4) The Baptist sects, which we shall discuss later, have from the beginning of their history most strongly and consistently maintained the principle that only those personally regenerated could be admitted to the Church. Hence they repudiated every conception of the Church as an institution (*Anstalt*) and every interference of the temporal power. Here also it was for positive religious reasons that unconditional toleration was advocated.

The first man who stood out for absolute toleration and the separation of Church and State, almost a generation before the Baptists and two before Roger Williams, was probably John Browne. The first declaration of a Church group in this sense appears to be the resolution of the English Baptists in Amsterdam of

1612 or 1613: "The magistrate is not to middle with religion or matters of conscience . . . because Christ is the King and Law-giver of the Church and conscience." The first official document of a Church which claimed the positive protection of liberty of conscience by the State as a right was probably Article 44 of the Confession of the Particular Baptists of 1644.

Let it be emphatically stated again that the idea sometimes brought forward, that toleration as such was favorable to capitalism, is naturally quite wrong. Religious toleration is neither peculiar to modern times nor to the West. It has ruled in China, in India, in the great empires of the Near East in Hellenistic times, in the Roman Empire and the Mohammedan Empires for long periods to a degree only limited by reasons of political expediency (which form its limits to-day also!) which was attained nowhere in the world in the sixteenth and seventeenth centuries. Moreover, it was least strong in those areas which were dominated by Puritanism, as, for instance, Holland and Zeeland in their period of political and economic expansion or in Puritan old or New England. Both before arid after the Reformation, religious intolerance was peculiarly characteristic of the Occident as of the Sassanian Empire. Similarly, it has prevailed in China, Japan, and India at certain particular times, though mostly for political reasons. Thus toleration as such certainly has nothing whatever to do with capitalism. The real question, Who benefited by it?

[H] The difference between this rational Pietist belief in Providence and its orthodox interpretation is shown characteristically in the famous controversy between the Pietists of Halle and the orthodox Lutheran Löscher. Löscher in his *Timotheus Verinus* goes so far as to contrast everything that is attained by human action with the decrees of Providence. On the other hand, Francke's consistent view was that the sudden flash of clarity over what is to happen, which comes as a result of quiet waiting for decision, is to be considered as "God's hint", quite analogous to the Quaker psychology, and corresponding to the general ascetic idea that rational methods are the way to approach nearer to God. It is true that Zinzendorf, who in one most vital decision entrusted the fate of his community to lot, was far from Francke's form of the belief in Providence. Spener, *Theologische Bedenken*, I, p. 314, referred to Tauler for a description of the Christian resignation in which one should bow to the divine will, and not cross it by hasty action on one's own responsibility, essentially the position of Francke. Its effectiveness as compared to Puritanism is essentially weakened by the tendency of Pietism to seek peace in this world, as can everywhere be clearly seen. "First righteousness, then peace", as was said in opposition to it in 1904 by a leading Baptist (G. White in an address to be referred to later) in formulating the ethical programme of his denomination (*Baptist Handbook*, 1904, p. 107).

[I] Which, however, had its limits. For this reason alone it is wrong to attempt to place Zinzendorf 's religion in a scheme of social psychological evolutionary stages, as Lamprecht does. Furthermore, however, his whole religious attitude is influenced by nothing more strongly than the fact that he was a Count with an outlook fundamentally feudal. Further, the emotional side of it would, from the point of view of social psychology, fit just as well into the period of the sentimental decadence of chivalry as in that of sensitiveness. If social psychology gives any clue to its difference from West European rationalism, it is most likely to be found in the patriarchal traditionalism of Eastern Germany.

J "That is a type of men who seek their happiness in four main ways: (1) to be insignificant, despised, and abased; (2) to neglect all things they do not need for the service of their Lord; (3) either to possess nothing or to give away again what they receive; (4) to work as wage laborers, not for the sake of the wage, but of the calling in the service of the Lord and their neighbor" (*Rel. Reden*, II, p. 180; Plitt, *op. cit.*, I, p. 445). Not everyone can or may become a disciple, but only those who receive the call of the Lord. But according to Zinzendorf's own confession (Plitt, op. cit., I, p. 449) there still remain difficulties, for the Sermon on the Mount applies formally to all. The resemblance of this free universality of love to the old Baptist ideals is evident.

K Though naturally it might interfere with it, as is to-day the case among the American Negroes. Furthermore, the often definitely pathological character of Methodist emotionalism as compared to the relatively mild type of Pietism may possibly, along with purely historical reasons and the publicity of the process, be connected with the greater ascetic penetration of life in the areas where Methodism is widespread. Only a neurologist could decide that.

L Naturally the Baptists have always repudiated the designation of a sect. They form *the* Church in the sense of the Epistle to the Ephesians v. 27. But in our terminology they form a sect not only because they lack all relation to the State. The relation between Church and State of early Christianity was even for the Quakers (Barclay) their ideal; for to them, as to many Pietists, only a Church under the Cross was beyond suspicion of its purity. But the Calvinists as well, *faute de mieux*, similarly even the Catholic Church in the same circumstances, were forced to favor the separation of Church and State under an unbelieving State or under the Cross. Neither were they a sect, because induction to membership in the Church took place *de facto* through a contract between the congregation and the candidates. For that was formally the case in the Dutch Reformed communities (as a result of the original political situation) in accordance with the old Church constitution

M How this principle was applied by the Quakers to seemingly trivial externals (refusal to remove the hat, to kneel, bow, or use formal address) is well known. The basic idea is to a certain extent characteristic of all asceticism. Hence the fact that true asceticism is always hostile to authority. In Calvinism it appeared in the principle that only Christ should rule in the Church. In the case of Pietism one may think of Spener's attempts to find a Biblical justification of titles. Catholic asceticism, so far as ecclesiastical authority was concerned, broke through this tendency in its oath of obedience, by interpreting obedience itself in ascetic terms. The overturning of this principle in Protestant asceticism is the historical basis of the peculiarities of even the contemporary democracy of the peoples influenced by Puritanism as distinct from that of the Latin spirit. It is also part of the historical background of that lack of respect of the American which is, as the case may be, so irritating or so refreshing.

N For not wealth alone, but also the impulsive pursuit of it (or what passed as such) was condemned with similar severity. In the Netherlands the South Holland Synod of 1574 declared, in reply to a question, that money-lenders should not be admitted to communion even though the business was permitted by law; and the Deventer Provincial Synod of 1598 (Art. 24) extended this to the employees of money-lenders. The Synod of Gorichem in 1606 prescribed severe and humiliating conditions under which the wives of usurers might be admitted, and the question was discussed as late as 1644 and 1657 whether Lombards should be admitted to communion (this against Brentano, who cites his own Catholic ancestors, although foreign traders and bankers have existed in the whole European and Asiatic world for thousands of years).

O The commandment of silence has been, starting from the Biblical threat of punishment for every useless word, especially since the Cluny monks, a favorite ascetic means of education in self-control. Baxter also speaks in detail of the sinfulness of unnecessary words.

P But this does not mean that the Puritan view-point was historically derived from the latter. On the contrary, it is an expression of the genuinely Calvinistic idea that the cosmos of the world serves the glory of God. The utilitarian turn, that the economic cosmos should serve the good of the many, the common good, etc., was a consequence of the idea that any other interpretation of it would lead to aristocratic idolatry of the flesh, or at least did not serve the glory of God, but only fleshly cultural ends.

Q Even in the Lutheran Confession of Duke Christopher of Württemberg, which was submitted to the Council of Trent, objection is made to the oath of poverty. He who is poor in his station should bear it, but if he swore to remain so it would be the same as if he swore to remain sick or to maintain a bad reputation.

R I think, among many other examples, especially of a manufacturer unusually successful in his business ventures, and in his later years very wealthy, who, when for the treatment of a troublesome digestive disorder the doctor prescribed a few oysters a day, could only be brought to comply with difficulty. Very considerable gifts for philanthropic purposes which he made during his lifetime and a certain openhandedness showed, on the other hand, that it was simply a survival of that ascetic feeling which looks upon enjoyment of wealth for oneself as morally reprehensible, but has nothing whatever to do with avarice.

S The reading of this passage may be recommended to all those who consider themselves today better informed on these matters than the leaders and contemporaries of the movements themselves. As we see, they knew very well what they were doing and what dangers they faced. It is really inexcusable to contest so lightly, as some of my critics have done, facts which are quite beyond dispute, and have hitherto never been disputed by anyone. All I have done is to investigate their underlying motives somewhat more carefully. No one in the seventeenth century doubted the existence of these relationships

T I should have thought that this sentence and the remarks and notes immediately preceding it would have sufficed to prevent any misunderstanding of what this study was meant to accomplish, and I find no occasion for adding anything. Instead of following up with an immediate continuation in terms of the above programme, I have, partly for fortuitous reasons, especially the appearance of Troeltsch's *Die Soziallehren der christlichen Kirchen und Gruppen*, which disposed of many things I should have had to investigate in a way in which I, not being a theologian, could not have done it; but partly also in order to correct the isolation of this study and to place it in relation to the whole of cultural development, determined, first, to write down some comparative studies of the general historical relationship of religion and society. These follow. Before them is placed only a short essay in order to clear up the concept of sect used above, and at the same time to show the significance of the Puritan conception of the Church for the capitalistic spirit of modern times.

CPSIA information can be obtained
at www.ICGtesting.com
Printed in the USA
LVHW041148091222
734813LV00005B/233